CHINA and ASIAN
REGIONALISM

CHINA and ASIAN REGIONALISM

Zhang Yunling

Chinese Academy of Social Sciences, China

World Scientific

NEW JERSEY · LONDON · SINGAPORE · BEIJING · SHANGHAI · HONG KONG · TAIPEI · CHENNAI

Published by

World Scientific Publishing Co. Pte. Ltd.

5 Toh Tuck Link, Singapore 596224

USA office: 27 Warren Street, Suite 401-402, Hackensack, NJ 07601

UK office: 57 Shelton Street, Covent Garden, London WC2H 9HE

British Library Cataloguing-in-Publication Data
A catalogue record for this book is available from the British Library.

ISBN-13 978-981-4282-22-2
ISBN-10 981-4282-22-7

Typeset by Stallion Press
Email: enquiries@stallionpress.com

Printed in Singapore.

Foreword

The East Asian cooperation movement started with sub-regional efforts led by Southeast Asian countries. ASEAN was established in the late 1960s with the aim of resisting external threats by uniting the regional members together. ASEAN readjusted its direction later by initiating AFTA and identifying the ASEAN Community as a goal. The great value of ASEAN is in uniting all members through regional cooperation to secure peace and promote the economic development of the Southeast Asian region. ASEAN, as a pioneer of the regional cooperation movement, also plays a very important role as a driver in leading East Asian countries toward regional cooperation. In 1997, ASEAN invited three major economies in Northeast Asia, i.e. China, Japan and the Republic of Korea, to dialogue and cooperate during the Asia financial crisis which started the process of the East Asian cooperation movement under the framework of "ASEAN+3".

A big step was made when "ASEAN+3" leaders agreed to set up a vision group of eminent persons from East Asia (EAVG) to envision the future of East Asian cooperation. The EAVG's report recommended that the long-term goal for East Asian cooperation should be an East Asia Community with high-level integration and cooperation on economics, politics, security, society and culture. Under the framework of East Asian cooperation, progress has been achieved in the areas of high-level policy dialogue and consultation (leaders' meetings, ministers' meetings, and other high officials' meetings), monetary and financial cooperation (Chiang Mai Initiative), FTAs (ASEAN+1 FTAs and feasibility study on East Asian FTA), as well as sub-regional cooperation (GMS). A new cooperative vehicle was also developed under the East Asia Summit (EAS) with the cooperation extending to India in South Asia and Australia and New Zealand in Oceania.

East Asia cooperation has developed within multi-layered frameworks, i.e. with several, rather than just one, integrated process. This may well comply with the reality of East Asia — a region with great diversity. However, the real challenge is how to make those different processes into an integrated single process, for example, from several "ASEAN+1 FTAs" into an EAFTA. ASEAN, with its long effort at regional cooperation, has decided to realize the ASEAN Community by 2015. Nevertheless, its role as a driver for the East Asia cooperation movement seems vulnerable due to its internal constraints. The question is: While supporting ASEAN's role as a driver and its effort towards building the ASEAN Community, how does it project and move forward the process of East Asia community-building? Also, the question is often raised about whether the East Asia cooperation movement really needs to be under a single and integrated process, and towards an East Asia Community. Europe, with its special and unique character of history, culture and politics, has developed a successful model from being a divided continent and becoming a united region based on very high-level integration in economics, politics and society. Although East Asia can learn a lot from the European experience, it has to define its own path and model in its effort towards becoming a community. ASEAN has spent 40 years in its effort towards becoming the ASEAN Community, while East Asia cooperation has began only about 10 years since. Compared with Europe, the history of regional cooperation in East Asia is still short. East Asian countries need both confidence and wisdom to drive the train of the regional cooperation movement rightly.

As a scholar, I am fortunate to participate directly and deeply in the East Asia cooperation process since the beginning as a member of EAVG and many other activities, such as the ASEAN–China

FTA Official Study Group, first general coordinator of Network of East Asia Think Tanks (NEAT), chairman of Joint Expert Group of Feasibility Study on EAFTA, the Joint Expert Group of Feasibility Study on CEPEA, etc. I have written intensively on all these areas in both Chinese and English. This book comprises 15 chapters and policy research reports in English on East Asia cooperation.

Contents

CHAPTER ONE

East Asian Cooperation: Path & Approach[1]

Introduction

East Asian Cooperation (EAC) has existed for more than 10 years. In 2001, the East Asian Vision Group (EAVG) for the first time called on "East Asia moving from a region of nations to a bona fide regional community with shared challenges, common aspirations, and a parallel destiny."[2] The recommendation was accepted by leaders of 10+3 countries by confirming "an East Asian community as a long-term objective that would contribute to the maintenance of regional and global peace, security, progress and prosperity."[3] Since then, progress has been made for East Asian cooperation, but the community-building has still a long way to go.

Europe has developed a unique model for community-building. East Asia is different from Europe and has to define its own model. Current East Asian economic integration has been built up mostly by market cooperation in following a multi-layered framework. EAC needs strong political will and a consolidated goal.

---

[1] This paper was written for China–ASEAN Think Tank Dialogue, Nanning, October 20–21, 2008.
[2] East Asian Vision report: Towards East Asian Community — Region of Peace, Prosperity and Progress, 2001.
[3] Chairman's Statement of the Ninth ASEAN Plus Three Summits, Kuala Lumpur, 12 December 2005.

1

With a multi-layered structure of regional cooperation, it is important that different efforts converge into an integrated roadmap. However, with the development of the East Asian Summit (EAS), the views on EAC seem to be more divided.

I. Emerging Regionalism

The foundation for East Asian regionalism has been built up mainly by regional economic integration. Currently, economic integration in East Asia has been deepened by a newly-developed production network. The network, based on exchange of trade, capital and technology, has profound impact on East Asian economic development since it has created a kind of "parallel development" for the economies in the region.

Economic integration in East Asia has been driven by: (1) Capital flow from more developed economies to less developed economies — firstly from Japan, then from the "four dragon" economies. Now, capital flows are more intersected among the economies, including those from developing economies to developed economies, which have facilitated capital and technology transfer and developed a vertical economic growth chain in East Asia. (2) Trade and FDI-friendly policy and open market strategy, i.e. liberalization of the markets by East Asian economies that have reduced transaction costs significantly and made the market-based economic integration easier. (3) China's economic rise, due to its great size and huge market potential, has become a new factor for regional economic growth and restructured the pattern of regional economic integration. China has become an important hub, both as a market for capital inflow, and a market for imports of goods and services. Based on the restructuring, a new regional production and service network has gradually been established.

Economic integration has created more and more shared interests, which has helped to develop a regional spirit and consciousness. The spirit of East Asian regionalism has been nurtured under an "ASEAN+" framework since the Asian financial crisis in 1997. The major framework is "ASEAN+3" which is not just an economic cooperation process. It also has political signifi-cance, i.e. helping to improve relations among the countries in the region. There are also the other frameworks — "ASEAN+1" and EAS — that serve as regional platforms for all members to engage and cooperate through dialogue and joint activities. However, EAC seems not to have a clear concept and identity yet.

II. East Asian Way

Current East Asian regionalism has shown its new characteristic feature that is more economic-centered, equally-participated and consensus-built.[4] Different from the EU model, it develops in an "East Asian way" that has witnessed the following characteristics:

(1) The institution will not develop into a regional organization with super-regional power. The regional cooperation is characterized more by a kind of "functional institution-building."[5] Gradualism and pragmatism are two important principles in the process of regional cooperation and integration. EAC building is based on shared interests, rather than a defined goal.[6]

(2) ASEAN, based on its pioneer experience for regional coopera-tion, plays a key role in bringing East Asia together as a region and shaping its direction. ASEAN provides a unique way (the ASEAN way) to bring all countries in Southeast Asian together gradually and to turn the region into a united and inte-grated one. The valuable spirit of ASEAN is to realize regional reconciliation through a gradual process based on functional cooperation. The ASEAN process is not just economic cooperation

---

[4] Dr. Prapat Thepchatree called it equality, consensus and comfort level, in *Towards an East Asian Community*, a paper presented at NEAT II, Bangkok, 2004, p. 5.

[5] Simon Tay suggested that the emerging East Asian sense of community be founded on a functional interdependence and institutional identity without excep-tionalism. Reader, Singapore Institute of International Affairs, 4(1), p. 32.

[6] EAVG report has well identified the aims of peace, prosperity and progress through a gradual process.

and integration, but also social and security community-building. The ASEAN way will be a vital influence on the path and approach of EAC.

(3) EAC building follows "open regionalism", i.e. pushing forward intra-regional cooperation and integration, while encouraging individual members or the sub-group to develop bilateral or sub-regional cooperation with outside members. While it allows the multi-layered frameworks in the region, it also recognizes the existing bilateral alliance or other agreements. Thus, the EAC building process is not intended to create an exclusive or inward-looking regional identity.[7]

(4) As the political motivation for East Asian cooperation is to improve regional relations and create peace for the long-term stability and prosperity of the region, rather than urging for a super-regional organization, the fundamental role of East Asian cooperation is to nurture more and more shared principles and rules for regional relations in a new international and regional setting.

III. Community Building

East Asian cooperation started from pragmatic need without a well-designed political goal, and to some extent, even without consensus building. Economic cooperation and integration provides a fundamental stake for East Asian regionalism.

Great diversity within the region is a key factor that needs to be addressed. EAC has to respect the differences while seeking for harmony, which means that it should not be setting up common values or principles for adoption by all members.[8]

---

[7] Mark Hong argues that East Asian regionalism was driven by market forces and guided by principles such as open regionalism, flexibility and liberalization. ASEAN community-building in the context of East Asian regionalism, a paper presented at NEAT II, p. 11.

[8] Some have argued that EAC should be based on common values such as human rights and representative democracy. See Hitoshi Tanaka, The "10+3" and East Asian Summit: A two-tiered approach to community-building. *East Asia Insights*, JECIE, No. 1, 2006.

EAC building is a comprehensive process that includes institutional-building in the economic, political and social areas. For the economic area, the most important progress should be achieved in realizing the East Asian FTA (EAFTA) and a regional financial architecture (further enhancement of the Chiang Mai Initiative and towards a regional financial fund). EAFTA should be rule-based and WTO-consistent, i.e. high level harmonization of the regional market. But in the political (and also security) area, the regional institution should be more flexible whose major role will be to help the members in the region for consolidation, reconciliation and cooperation, rather than super-intervention. In the social area, EAC needs to develop mechanisms for people to people exchanges, which will help to reduce the gaps and grievances and to develop a shared community spirit and culture. EAC needs public support.

East Asian institution-building has to overcome the difficulty of balancing the regional institutions and sub-regional formalities. For example, ASEAN's identity and role in East Asian institution-building must be respected, but ASEAN itself has to adjust to the new development in East Asia. As for East Asian political cooperation, it needs collective wisdom on how to define and establish East Asian political cooperation and security without hurting the existing relations both within the region and with those outside the region.[9]

The political significance of EAC is to realize regional political reconciliation and peace-making. Considering its great diversity, East Asia should find its own model for political unity with the principle of respecting the differences in political systems, social structures and culture.

The process of East Asian cooperation and integration plays a dual role in community-building: reconciliation among the

---

[9] Hitoshi Tanaka proposed that an East Asian security forum be set up, not to function as an alternative to existing blateral alliances, but to complement it. ARF should also continue to play a role. Tanaka: East Asia Community building: Towards an East Asia security forum. *East Asia Insights*, 2(21), 2007. JECIE, Tokyo.

countries, and cultivation of the members. EAC should play a positive role in mitigating the differences and reducing the tensions in the region, like the division and confrontation on the Korean Peninsula, Taiwan Straits relations, territory and island as well as Exclusive Economic Zone (EEZ) line disputes, and in helping to bring all members of the region into an integrated framework under its umbrella.

EAC faces many challenges. One of the factors for its progress is the real success of ASEAN community-building which gives ASEAN the confidence to continue to lead the region forward to be integrated into a larger regional architecture. Another is the China–Japan relationship. Although their relations have improved in recent years, they are not sharing a high-level strategy on regional community-building. As neither side will be accepted as the sole leader, their cooperation and joint efforts are crucial.[10] EAC will not be built up if China and Japan fail to share common interests and strategy, and to consolidate each other in the areas of EAFTA, financial cooperation, security strategy and regional institution-building.

Economic integration continues to be the key factor for East Asian cooperation and EAC building. Currently, East Asian countries are still busy with bilateral or sub-regional FTAs both within the region and outside of the region. An EAFTA (ASEAN+3) feasibility study has been conducted by the joint-expert group, which called on an early start of the EAFTA process, but has not been accepted by the leaders as an immediate action-oriented agenda. Another feasibility study for CEPEA (East Asia Summit-based framework) has also been finished but seems to be difficult for leaders to accept right now. ASEAN seems to have no strong interest to lead East Asia to an integrated FTA in either ASEAN+3 or East Asia Summit before the AEC is realized.

At present, the main concern of the regional members is how to deal with the global financial crisis that has led to the economic

---

[10] Simon Tay proposed that East Asian regionalism be led by issues since he argued that the region lacks a single leader who is both acceptable and able. Reader, p. 39.

slowdown. East Asian countries should strengthen their cooperation in macro-economic management and financial stability. In this
case, financial cooperation should move faster in establishing a
regional financial institution, for example, a regional fund for
financial stability.

IV. China's Policy and Role

As a big regional power, China should have a strong regional strategy.
The following factors should enable China to be positive towards
EAC:

(1) China has a vital economic stake in East Asia, with more than
60 percent of its foreign trade and capital inflow from the
region. Based on a regional production network in East Asia,
the Chinese economy has become an integrated part of the
regional economy. A liberalized, secure and stable regional
market is in China's interest, which encourages China to adopt
an active policy in participating and promoting RTAs, for
example, a China–ASEAN FTA, a proposed Northeast Asian
trilateral FTA and an EAFTA. China is also interested in participating and promoting regional monetary and financial
cooperation, like the Chiang Mai Initiative, and regional capital
market development, though with caution for a high-level institutional arrangement at this early stage.

(2) East Asia is a region that has vital geographical significance for
China. The "good neighbor policy" has become a principal
diplomacy for China to improve and strengthen its relations
with neighboring countries. This helps to create a long-term
peaceful environment for China's development and modernization. East Asian cooperation that brings countries in the
region together as a community will best serve both China's
economic and political interests.

(3) Although regionalism in East Asia is not intended to create an
exclusive bloc against any power, for example, the United States,
it may help to create a more balanced structure of regional and

global relations. The East Asian voice may be better addressed if the East Asian identity via EAC will be realized.

(4) China has a broad concept for regionalism since it is surrounded by different large geographical areas. Although China takes "10+3" (TPT) as the core course for EAC, it has a flexible attitude towards accepting and participating in the multi-layered frameworks, for example, EAS.[11] At the same time, China has made efforts in developing non-East Asian institutions, for example, SOC, the possible Northeast Asian security regime based on the success of Six-Party Talk.

(5) China's economic success has benefited from its global opening-up policy; thus China supports the WTO multilateral system. China also has a vital stake in the Asia-Pacific region, thus it is very interested to engage APEC and other Asia-Pacific initiatives, for example, in energy, financial cooperation, etc. From this perspective, China's regionalism is flexible and open-minded.

(6) China insists that East Asia should find its own way to cooperate. EAS does not intend to create an exclusive bloc by getting the US out. The US and East Asia have many channels for engagement and cooperation, for example, bilateral alliances and FTAs, APEC, ARF, as well as Six-Party Talk and the potential dialogue partner of SCO.

---

[11] The EAS has been identified by leaders as a strategic forum supporting EAC, but now it seems to have its own designs, like the Japan-proposed CEPEA, energy project etc. It is important that TPT and EAS are complementary.

CHAPTER TWO

Emerging East Asian Regionalism[1]

As a geographical concept, East Asia includes five countries in the northeast and 10 countries in ASEAN. As a region, it has gradually built up its common or shared interests in the economy, politics, security, society and culture, which constitute the foundation of "East Asian regionalism".

Nevertheless, great diversity, historical grievances, as well as some current contradictions among the countries in the region weaken the consensus of regionalism. East Asian regionalism is still very weak in building a real East Asian Community with a clearly-defined direction, approach and goal.

The great significance of East Asian cooperation and integration is its developing process. The process is irreversible which helps to create the consensus in searching for an appropriate approach and defining the long-term goal.

I. The Emergence of East Asian Regionalism

The idea of East Asian cooperation has a long history. In modern times, the Japanese were the ones who had put forward the concept of East Asian regionalism. By the late 19 century, Japan had

---

[1] This paper was written for the Conference on East Asian Regionalism and Its Impact. It was organized by the Institute of Asia-Pacific Studies, Chinese Academy of Social Sciences, in October 2004.

become the first industrial country in Asia. A rising Japan wanted to use regionalism to enlarge its interests in Asia and strengthen its status in dealing with other big powers. Thus, Japan was very active in mobilizing the spirit of "Asianism" and tried hard to establish an East Asian identity. But as the sole emerging power in East Asia, Japanese regionalism was nurtured with expansionism and ended as militarism.[2] In China, some early revolutionists also intended to call on East Asian unity to oppose Western colonization and to save China from being carved up by colonial powers. However, their voices were too weak to be influential. After the Second World War, East Asia was divided by international politics. The voice of East Asian regionalism vanished totally.

From the 1960s, the voice of economic regionalism in East Asia was raised again, firstly from Japan and then supported by the "Four Dragons".[3] But this time, it was characterized more by "Asia-Pacific regionalism", which aimed at establishing institutional linkage between Japan, other East Asian newly-emerging economies and the United States. Several forums were set up in the Asia-Pacific area then, like the Pacific Basin Economic Council (PBEC, 1967), the Pacific Trade and Development Conference (PAFTAD, 1968), the Pacific Economic Cooperation Council (PECC, 1980) and the Asia-Pacific Economic Cooperation (APEC, 1989).

In the early 1990s, there was a new call for East Asian regional cooperation. Dr. Mahathir Mohamad, then Prime Minister of Malaysia, called on East Asia to unite to balance the international economic order by "comprising economies in East Asia" and establishing an "East Asian Economic Group" (EAEG) in 1990, which was later changed to "East Asian Economic Caucus" (EAEC). His idea was not rootless since an emerging ASEAN and East Asia as a whole required a more favorable international economic system to reflect their interests. The proposal of establishing EAEC was

---

[2] See Wang Ping (2008). *Japan's Asianism in Modern History*, ShangWu Publisher, p. 55, 144, 25.

[3] Australia, together with Japan, played an important role in pushing the concept of the "Asia-Pacific" with the aim of identifying it as a member of the region.

supported by ASEAN since it could make ASEAN as the core of the organization to play a pivotal role in the process. However, Japan did not support such an initiative with an anti-Western background.[4]

Interestingly, East Asia as an economic region was firstly recognized by the international community in the early 1990s in a World Bank report, *East Asia Miracle*. Following this, East Asia was considered more and more as an integrated region based on its economic success. East Asia as a region first presented itself in world affairs in 1996 when ASEAN together with three northeast Asian countries, i.e. China, Japan and the Republic of Korea (ROK), known as ASEM, opened official dialogue with EU.

However, the real East Asian cooperation process only started after the Asian financial crisis. A historical step was made on 15 December 1997 in Kuala Lumpur when leaders from ASEAN, China, Japan and ROK got together to cooperate in dealing with the financial crisis and recovering the regional economies. A joint statement was announced by the leaders in the next year, which clearly indicated the shared interests in pushing forward East Asian cooperation. Following this statement, the annual leaders' informal meetings and ministers' meetings were formalized under a coordinated framework of "10+3". Although this was only a forum in nature, it began to nurture a new spirit of East Asian regionalism.

In a regional sense, financial cooperation achieved big progress with the "Chiang Mai Initiative" (CMI) which established a regional framework through "SWAP arrangements". This framework provides a foundation for further institutional development in the area of monetary and financial cooperation in the East Asian region.

In the trade and investment area, FTAs adopt a multi-layered approach: ASEAN FTA (AFTA), China–ASEAN FTA (CAFTA), Japan–Singapore Close Economic Partnership (JSCEP) and

---

[4] Sanae Suzuki (2004). East Asian cooperation through conference diplomacy: Institutional aspects of the ASEAN plus three (APT) framework. IDE–JETRO, p. 5.

Japan–Thailand, Japan–Philippines, Japan–Malaysia FTAs (undergoing negotiation), as well as intended Japan–ASEAN FTA (JAFTA) and ROK–ASEAN FTA (KAFTA). In theory, the benefits from an East Asian FTA (EAFTA) are much larger than any bilateral or a sub-regional one. Although it has not been on the leaders' agenda yet, it seems that pressure on starting EAFTA early has become strong, especially from the business community.[5]

As a matter of fact, the "10+3" framework is not just an economic cooperation process. It also has political significance in helping to improve relations among the countries in the region. "10+3" serves as a unique regional platform for all parties to engage and cooperate through dialogue and joint activities. China and ASEAN have significantly improved their relations in the process of establishing FTA and comprehensive economic partnerships. The two sides have now defined themselves as strategic partners. China, Japan and ROK started their informal leaders' dialogue annually under this framework, and a joint declaration on strengthening economic cooperation was issued in 2003 by the three countries for the first time in their history.

Based on this, a new concept, i.e. East Asia Community (EAC) has emerged and seems to be accepted by all sides.[6] EAC is both considered as a long-term goal and a gradual process for cultivating partnership among all parties in the region.

II. Development of East Asian Regionalism

From a pragmatic need without a well-designed political goal, and, even without consensus to some extent, the East Asian. Cooperation process seems to be gradually building up.

---

[5] China had announced that it would take the initiative to coordinate an academic study on the feasibility of EAFTA from 2005, and this proposal was supported by other East Asian leaders during the leaders' meeting in November 2004.

[6] EAC was firstly recommended by the East Asian Vision Group to "10+3" leaders in 2002. In 2003, Japan and ASEAN leaders formally called for the development of the East Asia Community in their joint statement.

Economic cooperation and integration provides a fundamental stake for East Asian regionalism. But high-level economic integration can only be achieved step by step due to the great differences among countries in the region. A fully liberalized and integrated East Asian big market needs at least more than a decade-long effort.

In facing current multi-layered efforts in building FTAs, it is necessary to consolidate them into the EAFTA. Based on the current three "10+1" FTAs formula (CAFTA, JAFTA, KAFTA), the rational choice is that EAFTA will be a combination of three "10+1" FTAs. Thus, the three "10+1" must be completed first. This is possible since ASEAN had announced that they would start negotiations with Japan and ROK from 2005 and complete them by 2007. If it follows this approach, EAFTA negotiation may start from 2008, finish by 2010, and complete by 2020.[7] This requires political determination of the leaders of the East Asian countries.

The success of developing EAFTA is essential. As mentioned above, it is desirable to design and initiate EAFTA early.[8] The significant role of EAFTA is to harmonize the East Asian market system through legal agreements according to recognized international standards. China and Japan should work together in forging an EAFTA, rather than competing "for leadership in East Asia and each maintaining its influence on ASEAN by promoting their own individual relations with ASEAN".[9]

The regional financial institution is an important part of the East Asian economic community. The Chiang Mai Initiative (CMI) provides a starting point based on bilateral SWAP arrangements

---

[7] Some less developed ASEAN members and some most sensitive sectors may be extended to 2025.

[8] Some Japanese experts had recommended that EAFTA be launched in 2005 and a treaty signed for East Asian Economic Community. See Japan's initiative for Economic Community in East Asia. *JFIR Report*, p. 9, June 2003.

[9] Sanae Suzuki, East Asian cooperation through conference diplomacy: Institutional aspects of the ASEAN plus Three framework. IDE working paper, 03/04(7), p. 13.

for East Asian financial cooperation, but this will go further. The further step is to establish the regional framework of the SWAP arrangements and, perhaps, also to enlarge its size. If this works, it is necessary to move it to a regional fund with the idea of pooling some of the large foreign reserves in East Asia. The main role of this fund is to back up the confidence of the financial market and to serve as rescue capital if any crisis emerges. Nevertheless, it should also help to enhance the regional financial institutions and the level of financial management.

The political significance of East Asian regionalism is to realize regional political reconciliation and peace-making. Considering its great diversity, East Asia should find its own model for political unity, with the principle of respecting differences in political systems, social structures and culture.

The regional institutional-building needs to be strengthened. A further step from current the "10+3" dialogue framework to the East Asia Summit (EAS) and then possibly to a regional organization (for example, East Asian Organization[10]) seems necessary. Its major role is peace-making through cooperation under a regional framework. For this purpose, the region does not need just security dialogue, but also a security mechanism. In fact, a pivotal role for the process of East Asian cooperation is that East Asian countries learn to live together peacefully and manage the rules for their relationships.

In forging an integrated approach for current multi-layered processes, it should not end up as an existing sub-regional institution like ASEAN. However, it will have to coordinate all individually-initiated programs into an East Asian framework, rather than to allow each to compete with the other.

The development of East Asian regionalism has to overcome many difficulties. Great diversity within the region is clearly an obstacle since economic integration is based on high-level economic convergence. For example, EAFTA will have to respect

---

[10] The same group of Japanese experts proposed the establishment of the "Organization for East Asia" (OEA). *JFIR Report*, p. 9, June 2003.

the different economic interests, on the one hand, and establish a standard liberalization system for the regional market, on the other hand.

East Asian integration and market liberalization have started from sub-regional and bilateral arrangements. The East Asian institution-building has to overcome the difficulty of balancing regional institutions and sub-regional formalities. For example, ASEAN's identity and role in East Asian institution-building must be respected, but ASEAN itself has to adjust to the new development in East Asia. Furthermore, East Asian regionalism includes political cooperation. This needs collective wisdom on how to define and establish East Asian political cooperation and security without hurting the existing relations both within the region and outside the region.

A key factor for the progress of East Asian regionalism is China–Japan relations. The East Asian identity will not be built up if China and Japan fail to share common interest and consolidate each other in the EAFTA, financial cooperation, security strategy and regional institution-building. The current "cooling atmosphere" in political relations between China and Japan has certainly hurt the progress of East Asian regionalism.

China's active participation and role are also crucial in pushing East Asian regionalism. Nevertheless, China has to clear its own house at the same time. The Taiwan issue does not only influence China's role, but the whole East Asian community. China will not allow Taiwan to be involved if its government will not give up its pro-independence policy, and a regional community will not be realized if China and the region fail to find an acceptable way to let Taiwan be part of the regional community process. The division and confrontation on the Korean Peninsula is another factor that should not be underestimated.

As a matter of fact, the process of East Asian cooperation and integration plays a dual role in community-building: reconciliation among the countries (new partnership), and cultivation of every member (towards a new mindset). However, we have already witnessed some new developments in East Asian regionalism.

A significant step forward is the understanding and acceptance of the "East Asian Community" recommended by the "East Asian Vision Group" (EAVG).[11] This has been reinforced by pushing forward the "10+3" dialogue structure into an "East Asia Summit".[12] If this is to be realized, the embryonic identity of East Asian regionalism will be created.

The current East Asian regionalism has shown its new characteristic feature. Thus, we may call them as "new East Asian regionalism". The current process of new regionalism is economic-centered, equally participated and consensus built,[13] which is totally different from the ancient and modern regional order. We have already found some new features in this process:

Firstly, the institutional building will not intend to develop a regional organization with super-regional power. The regional cooperation is more characterized by a kind of "functional institutional building. Gradualism and pragmatism are two important principles in the process of regional cooperation and integration. The functional mechanism will help to build up the foundation of East Asian regionalism.

Secondly, the new East Asian regionalism finds its embryonic structure in ASEAN. ASEAN provides a unique way (the ASEAN way) to bring all countries gradually in Southeast Asian region together and to turn the region from a divided one into a united and integrated one. The valuable spirit of ASEAN is to realize the regional reconciliation through a gradual process based on functional cooperation. ASEAN becomes a pioneer in developing regionalism in East Asian region. ASEAN process is not just the economic cooperation and integration, but also the political and security community building. It has plaid a key role in bringing Southeast Asia and Northeast Asia together. The ASEAN way may

---

[11] Towards an East Asian Community: Region of peace, prosperity and progress. *East Asian Vision Group Report*, 2001.

[12] The summit was held in 2005.

[13] Dr. Prapat Thepchatree called it equality, consensus and comfort level, in Towards an East Asian Community, a paper presented NEAT II, Bangkok, 2004, p. 5.

be the major approach in the development of new East Asian regionalism.

Thirdly, the new East Asian regionalism will follow a kind of "new open regionalism", i.e. while pushing forward intra-regional cooperation and integration, also encouraging individual members or the sub-group developing bilateral or sub-regional cooperation with outside members. Economically, it allows a multi-layered FTA process, while in the political and security, recognizing the existing bilateral alliance or other agreements. Thus, East Asian regionalism will not intend to create an exclusive or inward looking regional identity.

Fourthly, the political motivation of East Asian cooperation is to improve regional relations and to create peace for the long-term stability and prosperity of the region, rather than urging for a super regional organization. However, gradual institutional building on a regional level is an integrated part of East Asian regionalism. The fundamental role of East Asian cooperation and following institutional progress is to make principles and rules for the regional relations in a new international and regional setting, which provides a platform for East Asian countries to live together peacefully and cooperate for prosperity based on the equal participation and shared interests for the first time in the long history. The roles of China and Japan are crucial in securing the progress of East Asian community building. But it seems neither side will be accepted as the sole leader.[14]

East Asian regionalism is still in its early stage. The above trends are not setting principles, but some important shared understandings. East Asian regionalism will continue to develop and enrich its programs. However, to secure its successful development, East Asians must find their own approach, i.e. an "East Asian way".

---

[14] Simon Tay proposed that East Asian regionalism be led by issues since he argued that the region lacks a single leader who is both acceptable and able. Reader, Singapore Institute of International Affairs, Vol. 4, No. 1, p. 39.

III. The Role of East Asian Regionalism

Europe has provided a successful model in consolidating a divided region through regional cooperation and integration. EU has become a super regional institution to manage regional economic, political and social affairs. The valuable EU experience for East Asia is that regional integration helps to realize reconciliation and peace, and the key of community-building is the regional institution-building. East Asia will not copy the EU model, but it also needs gradual institution-building in its own way.

An important role for the East Asian cooperation and integration process is to make rules and develop the legal mechanism among countries in the region through all kinds of arrangements. These arrangements and agreements both at the bilateral or subregional levels are rules made according the principle of international standards, or which are "WTO-consistent". In East Asian relations, this has profound significance since both "rule of standards" and "rule of law" will help to improve the systems of the regional members and to create a reliable foundation for the regional cooperation process.

East Asian cooperation and integration will help to develop a new regional order based on increasingly common or shared interests among all parties. China and Japan will find greater difficulty in managing their relations in a changing situation of "a rising China" and "a normalized Japan" if there is no common framework binding the two countries together. The two may find a larger space to be together under the East Asian community-building, and pressure from the others will also help to prevent the two from competing for its own influence or leadership.

East Asian institution-building creates the "public property" for regional countries to maximize their interests. In a context of globalization, East Asian regionalism may help to identify its regional role and strive for its interests, which also helps to create a more balanced world order.

New East Asian regionalism is still weak due to its short history and embryonic structure. East Asia may need a longer time to realize its dream of building an East Asian Community compared to Europe. But the train of regional cooperation has started to move and the moving process itself has its value.

CHAPTER THREE

Projecting East Asian Community-Building[1]

T he concept of the East Asian Community has been accepted as an institutional architecture of East Asian cooperation, which represents a significant progress of emerging East Asian regionalism. However, East Asian regionalism is still in a framework of "10+3" and a multi-layered economic liberalization process. Compared with Europe and North America, East Asia is moving slowly towards an integrated approach of regional institution-building. Instead it should be speeding up its process of regional cooperation and community-building.

I. What Can We Learn from the European and American Experiences?

EU's most valuable contribution is that peace and prosperity have been secured through its process of cooperation and integration. The following three major experiences are the most valuable lessons:

Political reconciliation: Two World Wars made Europe highly divided. The European cooperation process provided a single and genuine framework to bring the forever enemies together in working for the shared and increasingly common interests.

---

[1] This is a policy report written for the Second Network of East Asian Think-Tanks (NEAT) annual conference in Bangkok in March 2004.

Institution-building: A gradual and steady institutional design helped make Europe really integrated. From European Coal and Steel Union to the European Common market, European Economic Community to the European Community and finally the European Union — all these have progressed for a half century.

Balanced interests: During the liberalization and integration process, the interests of less competitive sectors and less developed economies were specially considered and protected through well-designed arrangements and rules.

The significance of European regionalism is that all European countries have been gradually absorbed into a united and highly integrated greater Europe, by a single market, a single currency, as well as a single super political organization. This is a big challenge to the other parts of the world since European countries can act as a single powerful group to gain and defend their best interests.

The three North American countries have realized their integration mainly through NAFTA. The nature of NAFTA is to integrate the market through comprehensive coverage of sectors and regulation arrangements. NAFTA provides a unique case for integrating a most developed economy (the US) with a developing economy (Mexico). The experience of NAFTA shows that a less developed economy can also gain from participating in regional liberalization arrangements. NAFTA will expand itself into FTAA in the coming years, which will combine North America, Central America and Latin America into a single liberalized market. If it happens, this will significantly reshape the structure of the world market.

In East Asia, the regional cooperation and integration effort is pioneered by ASEAN. Almost at the same time that the EU launched its single market, North America started NAFTA and ASEAN launched its AFTA. ASEAN plays an important role in bridging the Southeast and Northeast Asian regions together under the framework of "10+3" (ASEAN 10 and China, Japan and

Republic of Korea (ROK). What we need urgently now is to project an integrated approach of East Asian community-building.

Determination, pragmatism and wisdom are probably three key words we should keep in mind in studying the experiences of EU and NAFTA. East Asia will lose out and fail to play its role as a powerful region in leading global economic dynamism and also in reshaping world relations in the international arena if it moves too slowly to integrate itself.

II. How Should We Define Ourselves?

The East Asian Vision Group (EAVG) in its report recommended that the long-term goal for East Asian cooperation and integration is an East Asian Community. It seems that the concept of the "East Asian Community" has been commonly accepted. However, the real challenge for us is how to define ourselves.

What is the foundation for an East Asian Community? The simple answer is that we share common interests, not just economically, but also politically. East Asian regionalism started mostly from economic integration and cooperation. Nevertheless, the process goes well beyond economic areas. For the long-term peace and prosperity of the region, we need regional institutions.

The great value of East Asian regionalism is the process of participation, conciliation and cooperation for the members of the region. East Asia may not go to a European-style union, but gradual institutionalization is absolutely necessary. EU and NAFTA provide two different models for regional integration; East Asia has to find its own way.

ASEAN is a pathfinder in developing regional convergence in East Asia. The ASEAN experience illustrates that differences are not decisive obstacles to regional integration. The Asian value favors the philosophy of "harmony but with differences". The current "10+3" process provides a general framework for East Asian countries to be together. It gives birth to a consciousness and structure of East Asian regionalism.

The function of East Asian regionalism is to bind all members of the region together based on agreements and institutions. It is to secure peace and development through cooperation. East Asian regionalism does not intend to create a super organization for regional governance and is not exclusive. It needs cooperation with other parties based on its own institutional identity, but this does not mean that we should not have our own regional identity. East Asians should be confident enough to define themselves with a real identity. An East Asian open regionalism would mean that the region will make all efforts to develop cooperative relations with other partners along with community-building.

III. What Should be Done Now and in the Near Future?

Firstly, we should strengthen regional institution-building at a high level. It is very important to move the current "10+3" process into an East Asian identity. There are two options:

Option one: To have a new Leaders Declaration on East Asian Community in 2005, or at least in 2007 (a 10th anniversary of East Asian cooperation), indicating the aim, goal and principle of community-building.[2] East Asian institution-building will follow the functional approach, not for a super-national power organization. This is different from the European model.

Option two: As a first step of East Asian community-building, to set up a regional organization, for example, "Organization of East Asian Cooperation" (OEAC) by 2007. However, considering great differences in East Asia, OEAC will not be a regional organization with super-national authority at the beginning, but a regional "functional vehicle" for coordinating and promoting of cooperation developments.

Secondly, while encouraging all existing multi-layered FTA efforts, preparation for the East Asian FTA (EAFTA) should be

---

[2] The first leaders' statement was in 1999. See *Joint Statement on East Asia Cooperation*, 28 November 1999.

done early. Leaders should consider setting up an official expert group to start the feasibility study in 2005 and present its recommendations in 2006. EAFTA should be completed earlier than 2020.

Thirdly, further steps should be taken in strengthening financial cooperation through doubling the size of SWAP arrangements under the Chang Mai Initiative (CMI) and advancing it into a common regional financial architecture. It is necessary to set up an expert group to start a feasibility study for a regional monetary fund.

Additionally, other areas of work include, e.g., has part of community-building, setting up a functional mechanism for non-traditional security cooperation; launching an East Asian education program for the aim of setting up student exchange programs and East Asia teaching programs among East Asian universities; launching an East Asian business travel card program and an electronic East Asian tourism network, etc.

The value of East Asian community-building is its process, i.e. the comprehensive participation and cooperation of nations in the region with real actions. There is no a ready model for East Asia to copy. The region must find its own model and approach under the principle of gradualism and pragmatism.

IV. The Nature of East Asian Community-Building

The East Asian Community will be built on three pillars:

The first pillar is high-level institution-building. Community-building needs institutions. East Asia cooperation has been conducted under a "10+3" framework. It naturally moves to an integrated regional approach with institutional structures, for example, an East Asian Summit for top-level dialogue and cooperation, councils for functional coordination, and, perhaps, a regional organization for coordination, rather than management.

The second pillar is a closely integrated regional economic partnership. While encouraging the current multi-layered efforts in bilateral FTAs, it is important to develop an East Asian Close

Economic Partnership Framework Agreement (EACEP), then an EAFTA. EACEP does not just promote liberalization, but also economic cooperation. Cooperation and shared prosperity should be the central value for East Asian economic relations.

The third pillar is the political and security arrangement. A key role of the East Asian Community is to realize the region's long-term peace. The peace-making can only be realized through cooperation. Considering its great diversity, East Asia should find its own model for political built-up, while insisting on the principle of respecting differences in political systems, social structures and cultures, and also supporting gradual institutional development at the same time. For example, it is necessary to start the defense ministers' meeting along with other ministerial meetings and to set up the East Asian Security Forum early.

The major role of the regional institutional building is peace-making through cooperation under a regional framework. The regional political and security mechanism will provide East Asian countries with a unique platform to learn how to live together peacefully based on shared interests and rules. The development of East Asian political security does not need defining a common enemy and will not be against other existing systems. It is supplementary to existing institutions and systems.

The key role for East Asian cooperation and integration process is to make rules and to develop the legal mechanism among countries in the region through arrangements and agreements. The significance of those arrangements and agreements, even including the bilateral or sub-regional ones, is the rule making in consisting international standards (economically, for example, "WTO consistent") and rules. In East Asian relations, this has profound impact since both "rule of standards" and "rule of law" will help to improve the systems of the regional members and to create a reliable foundation for the regional relations.

East Asian cooperation started without a clearly defined goal. Its great value is the process itself. This process will create more and more shared understanding, shared views, shared interests and shared rules for the countries in the region. Thus, the process of East Asian cooperation and integration will help to develop a new regional order and secure long-term prosperity. This new regionalism will help to nurture new relations.

The ASEAN way is often criticized as too soft. But it really provides a unique way to bring all countries in the Southeast Asian region together through the process of dialogue, reconciliation, coordination and gradual institutional development. ASEAN is a pathfinder in nurturing regional cooperation in East Asia. It is ASEAN that brought the three Northeast Asian countries together and initiated the "10+3" process. Its experience provides a useful paradigm for East Asian community-building though the EAC will have to do more than ASEAN.

To turn the current "10+3" dialogue framework into an "East Asian structure" needs wisdom. To start the East Asian Summit in 2005, it will face three difficulties:

One is the role of ASEAN. ASEAN wishes to continue to play the pivotal role in the future since it worries that it may be sidelined if the community is led by the big powers, i.e., either China or Japan.

Second is the membership. Some non-East Asian countries have shown their strong interest to join.

Third is its structure and role. "10+3" is still in an early stage of development. Is it proper to replace it by an East Asia Summit (EAS)?

To overcome the first difficulty, it is desirable to encourage ASEAN to continue to play its role as a center to bridge and bring all parties together. ASEAN's concern and initiative should be respected. Both China and Japan should announce their support of ASEAN's leading role.

To overcome the second difficulty, the members of EAS should be restricted to the geographical countries of East Asia. If alternatively, it should be extended to India, Australia and New Zealand, the nature of EAS may be adjusted to a platform for East Asian cooperation with non-East Asian countries. By so doing, it may continue the "10+3" leaders' annual meeting.

The above measures are closely related to overcoming the third difficulty, i.e., EAS is considered as an extension of East Asian cooperation, and from a future perspective, the East Asia cooperation process may follow a multi-layered structure in the long term. Thus, East Asian community-building will be seen as a cooperation movement with many functional developments within a united regional organization.

References

Austria, M. S. (2003). East Asian Regional Cooperation: Approaches and Processes. Discussion Papers 2003-02. Philippine Institute for Development Studies.

Cai, K. G. (2003). The ASEAN–China Free Trade Agreement and East Asian regional grouping. *Contemporary Southeast Asia*.

Chen, E. K. Y. (2001). *East Asia Economic Cooperation: China's Viewpoint*. NPF. www.old.npf.org.tw

Hamada, K., Matsushita, M. and Komura, C. (2000). *Dreams and Dilemmas*, Seikei University.

Pasadilla, G. (2004). East Asian Cooperation: The ASEAN View. Philippine Institute for Development Studies. Discussion Papers 2004-27.

Sekiguchi, N. M. (1999). *Road to ASEAN 10*. JCIE.

Tian, Z. (2003). East Asian cooperation and China's strategic interest. *Contemporary Asia-Pacific Studies*, 5.

Yi, W. "East Asia Cooperation Promising." (23 August 2002) *People's Daily*.

Yoshihide, S. (2002). Functional cooperation in East Asia. www.highbeam. com/doc

Zhang, Y. (2003a). East Asian Cooperation: The Approach and Direction. *China and World Economy*, 1.

Zhang, Y. (2003b). East Asian Cooperation: Progress and Future. Beijing: World Affairs Press.

Zhu, R. (2002). Joint Efforts to Promote East Asian Cooperation to A New Stage. Speech at the Sixth Summit of ASEAN, China, Japan and ROK, Phnom Penh.

CHAPTER FOUR

East Asian Cooperation: Where is it Going?[1]

Enamely 10 ASEAN countries plus China, Japan and the
Republic of Korea (ROK), has received increasing attention.
Since it was formalized in 1997, notable achievements have been
made: an institutional framework for regional cooperation has
been set up through annual leaders', ministers' and senior officials'
meetings; real progress in financial cooperation via the Chiang Mai
Initiative; preferential trade arrangements (PTA), like AFTA,
China–ASEAN FTA initiative, Japan–Singapore (closer economic
partnership (CEP), as well as sub-regional development projects.

However, the progress of East Asian cooperation is still considered to be limited. The real question is: how far can it go and
what kind of model will it follow?

I. From Division to Convergenc

There has been no unilaterally accepted culture or civilization for
the East Asian region after the collapse of the "Middle kingdom
order" as early as the 14th century. The later colonization of
Southeast Asia and the wars in the northeast region created disorder

---

[1] This paper was presented on the conference on East Asian Cooperation: Progress
and Future organized by Institute of Asia-Pacific Studies, Chinese Academy of
Social Sciences in Beijing in September 2002.

in East Asia for a long time. From the early 20th century, Japan, as a rising power tried to stamp its own order under the so-called "Great East Asian Co-Prosperity Sphere" but failed. The end of World War II divided the East Asian region into two separated blocs and markets. China played a unique role in bridging this division when it decided to move away from the Soviet bloc and reform its economic system and open up to the West in the late 1970s. In a gradual transition, the East Asian region became more or less integrated due to the end of the Cold War, the regional economic dynamism and close economic interconnections.

Economic convergence has emerged mainly from a "flying geese" model led by Japan from the 1960s, then followed by the "four dragons" (ROK, Singapore, Hong Kong, Taiwan), and some Southeast Asian countries, and lately by China. This model helped to build up a "vertical" chain through capital flow, technological transfer and supply of manufacturing parts, thus formulating a high-level intra-regional integration based on market exchange. Until the mid-1990s, intra-regional trade in East Asia was as high as more than 50 percent.

During that period of time, Japan did not take the lead to promote regional preferential trade arrangement. Instead ASEAN initiated the AFTA as early as in 1992. The 1997 financial crisis was an important turning point since it changed both the environment and the structure of East Asian economic growth and integration.

Firstly, due to a decade-long stagnation of its economy and also the negative effects of the Asian financial crisis, Japan was no longer the "locomotive" of East Asian economic growth which disrupted the "flying geese" model.

Secondly, the Southeast Asian region was plunged into serious recession because of the financial crisis and political instability.

Thirdly, China became the positive factor in stabilizing and revitalizing the regional economy since it was spared the financial crisis and kept its currency stable.

Not surprisingly, in the aftermath of the financial crisis, a new push for regional cooperation emerged, leading to the first "ASEAN plus three" (China, Japan and ROK) (APT) leaders' meeting in Kuala Lumpur in November 1997. The aim of the meeting was clear: achieving early economic recovery and preventing another crisis. This is a very important historical event since it opened the way for a real regional cooperation process based on regional interests and a newly-defined regional identity, i.e., that of East Asia.

This East Asian convergence goes beyond market integration by desiring governmental cooperation and institution-building.[2] As a matter of fact, regionalism finds its rationale in not just economic benefits, but also political interests. Europe is a leader in forging high-level regional integration. North America turned to regional free trade arrangement (RTA) from the early 1990s and achieved great success by concluding the North American Free Trade Agreement (NAFTA) in 1994. A broad FTA covering the whole of North, Central and Latin America — "free trade agreement of Americas" (FTAA) — was also put on the agenda. East Asia is comparatively late in forging regional RTA and other institutional establishments. Aside from intra-regional desire for a closer partnership, East Asian new regionalism is also considered to be a rational response to the progress of other regions, especially to the establishment of NAFTA.[3] By definition, East Asian economic integration started as early as from the 1960s, based on regional economic growth but only by market approach, while the process of regional cooperation through regional institutional arrangement through governmental efforts began only from the late 1990s. East Asian market-based integration has its vulnerability. Thus, this new initiative for regional cooperation will certainly

---

[2] Shujiro Urata argued for "a shift from market-led to institution-led regional economic integration in East Asia", in a paper prepared for the Conference on Asian Economic Integration organized by Research Institute of Economy, Trade and Industry, Tokyo, April 22–23, 2002, p. 1.

[3] Prime Minister Mahathir's proposal of forming the East Asian Economic Caucus (EAEC) has been considered to be a direct response to NAFTA. Peter Drysdale & Kenichi Ishigaki. (ed.). East Asian Trade and Financial Integration: New issues. Canberra: Asia-Pacific Press. 2002, p. 6.

help to enhance and facilitate further integration of the East Asian region.

However, as a process of regional cooperation and integration, there are still many unfavorable factors. Political disarray separates many countries and fosters distrust. For example, there is still a long way to go before China and Japan can become real partners. At the same time, confrontation and tension in the Korean Peninsula and the Taiwan Straits leave the East Asia region in a situation of uncertainty and instability. To some extent, East Asia is still divided in its regional security. Economic convergence will surely help to bridge the gap and create new ties, but political distrust and security issues, if without special effort, may slow down or even obstruct the cooperation process.

II. Progress of East Asia Cooperation

The East Asian cooperation process formally started on 15 December 1997 when the first meeting of the leaders of APT was held in Kuala Lumpur, the capital of Malaysia, against the backdrop of the financial crisis. The dialogue focused on how to overcome the financial crisis and spur economic recovery through regional cooperation. Since then, the annual leaders' meeting has continued and noticeable achievements have been made in many areas.

APT has become the major course of the East Asian cooperation process. Thus, an integrated framework for East Asian cooperation is emerging. The annual leaders' meeting has become a major mechanism for official dialogue and consultation on immediate and long-term regional issues ranging from economics macroeconomic policy, sub-regional development to political stability and security. There are four tracks of leaders' meeting, i.e. ASEAN 10, ASEAN+1 (China, Japan and South Korea separately), Northeast Asia 3 (China, Japan and ROK) and ASEAN+3. Each group identifies its own priorities for discussion and cooperation. For example, China, Japan and ROK leaders' meeting was formalized to coordinate and support the APT process and also to discuss important issues relating to their own interests. Aside from the three leaders' meeting, economic and trade ministers also meet independently. The China–ASEAN FTA was discussed in 2000 and agreed on in 2001 within the ASEAN + China track. Importantly, APT enables East Asian leaders to exchange views on regional issues and build consensus on crucial policy coordination.

Ministers' meetings provide regional coordination in increasing areas which include meetings, of foreign ministers, trade ministers and finance ministers. Their two major functions are: to prepare the agendas for the leaders' meeting and to discuss issues of regional concern. Macro-economic policy dialogue is one of the most important areas for exchange of information and consolidation of policies among East Asian countries. Financial cooperation based on the Chiang Mai Initiative (CMI) was first discussed and agreed on by financial ministers in Chiang Mai, Thailand in 2000 and then submitted to the leaders' meeting.

Senior officials meet to prepare for both ministers' and leaders' meetings at the working level, as do task forces and functional forums, like "East Asian Vision Group" (EAVG), "East Asian Study Group" (EASG), "Industrial and Business Forum" etc. More task forces are set up as the need arises.

The above framework consolidates all activities into the APT process.[4] It moves beyond mere policy consultations since some real institutional arrangements are developed. Among them, the CMI, i.e. swap arrangements among East Asian countries, is the most significant, which may help further a higher level of financial and monetary integration for East Asia.

However, APT is still an "ASEAN plus" process, a cooperative framework forged by multi-layered processes conducted by different countries, or different groups of countries, in the region. The partners have different aims, ways, means and directions.

ASEAN is a pathfinder in promoting regional integration and cooperation and has a unique role in bridging East Asian countries into the East Asian cooperative process. But it does not seem ready

---

[4] This does not prevent any country or a group of countries at the same time from cooperating or signing FTA with other countries within or without APT.

to accept a unilateral identity of East Asia since this may end its special leverage as an initiator or leader in regional affairs. So the proposal made by the EAVG to turn the APT leaders' meeting to the "East Asian Summit" seems a challenge to ASEAN.

Japan, as the largest economy in the region, is a key factor in any regional arrangement. Japan has moved in a new direction by initiating and concluding bilateral FTAs, but "a comprehensive deal is not on with Japan because of agriculture",[5] neither for a bilateral nor a regional deal. Prime Minister Koizumi's proposal for a broad regional FTA including APT members, India, Australia and New Zealand was considered only as a political response to the China–ASEAN FTA initiative. It is clear that Japan is not yet ready to move to an East Asian strategy on FTA.

China has become active in joining the regional arrangement after its accession of the WTO. A surprising move is its initiative to forge a FTA with ASEAN. This shows its new interest and confidence in regional cooperation. Nevertheless, China's regional strategy is mixed with enthusiasm in some areas and conservatism in others. Due to its own political concerns and the complexity of the Taiwan issue, China is even more reluctant to encourage regional institutional establishment in politics and security.

ROK has played an active role in moving toward an East Asian identity by proposing the EAVG and EASG, but is in fact not ready to accept a comprehensive FTA on a regional level due to its protective agricultural policy. President Kim Dae-jung had intended to bring North Korea into the East Asian cooperation process, but this would certainly take time.

China, Japan and ROK are all in the Northeast Asian region which accounts for the majority of East Asian GDP and trade. But due to big differences in economic structure and political distrust, this sub-region has failed to play a leading role in promoting the East Asian FTA or a comprehensive strategy for regional integration. Although China, Japan and ROK started their leaders' meeting

---

[5] Peter Drysdale & Kenichi Ishigaki (2001), p. 5.

under the APT process, China and Japan are far from being partners in forging regional identity.

At the same time, the real progress of some projects for cooperation, like the Great Mekong sub-regional development project (GMS), is very limited. Even well-mentioned swap arrangements in the name of CMI have been conducted slowly. A regional scheme in this area has not been designed yet.

However, the APT process, like a moving train, is already on its way. APT has been observed to be "not as a regional trading arrangement, but rather seeking to provide a framework for demonstrating East Asian leadership and influence on regional and international affairs".[6] The question then follows: where is this train going and what is the next station?

III. Direction and Model

The third leaders' meeting held in Manila on 28 November 1999 was an important turning point for the APT process because for the first time "the Joint Statement on East Asia Cooperation" was made public by the leaders. The statement listed focal points for cooperation in the economic, social, political and security areas.[7]

Economic cooperation was stated as the major area. Accelerating regional trade, investment and technology transfer were greatly emphasized. In order to gain regional economic stability and sustainable growth, the leaders even considered establishing an "East Asia economic council". Monetary and financial cooperation was given special weight in view of the financial crisis, and the APT framework was recognized as a major mechanism for regional cooperation. Moreover, to make regional cooperation as a process of community-building, the leaders also stressed the importance of regional cultural exchanges and dialogue and cooperation in the political and security fields.[8]

---

[6] Peter Drysdale & Kenichi Ishigaki (2001), p. 8.
[7] Leaders Joint Statement on East Asian Cooperation, Manila, 28 November 1999.
[8] Joint Statement on East Asian Cooperation, Manila, 1999.

APT has shown itself as a value-added process. There have been new projects every year since 1999. However, the major concern remains: what is the direction of this process? The answer can be found in the key recommendations made by EAVG:[9]

(1) To establish an "East Asian Free Trade Area (EAFTA)".
(2) To turn the current APT leaders' annual meeting into "the East Asian Summit".
(3) To coordinate macroeconomic policy and financial market regulations, cooperate in monitoring capital flows, build self-help and support mechanisms, and work towards capital market development and eventually monetary integration in the region.
(4) To promote coordination and joint action to combat common challenges such as drug trafficking, piracy, illegal migration, environmental disasters, money laundering, international terrorism and other trans-boundary crimes.
(5) To set up a regional organization, consisting of both existing national and regional scientific organizations, to identify and coordinate science and technology activities in the East Asian region.
(6) To provide a strong mandate for the creation of an institutional mechanism for regional cooperation, with the ultimate goal of the establishment of a regional entity — "East Asia Community (EAC)".

This is the first clearly spelt-out long-term vision for East Asia. However, these recommendations were not immediately accepted when they were presented to the APT leaders' meeting in 2001. This was understandable since it seemed premature to advocate an EAFTA or even an EAC in this early process.

Considering the great diversity of the East Asian region and the complexity of relations among the countries, the following

---

[9] East Asian Vision Group Report, 2001.

strategies could be adopted in promoting the process of East Asian cooperation and integration:

(1) To adopt a pragmatic approach.
(2) To encourage multi-layered arrangements and gradually move to a unique regional framework.
(3) To separate economic from political and security cooperation.

There is no consensus on the final goal of regional cooperation though the process train is already on the way. Great differences in economic development, political systems and security concerns prevent movement on a fast track. Therefore, the above strategies may be the only feasible way for continuous progress.

A pragmatic approach means that East Asian cooperation should select "what needs to be done and what can be done". For the purpose of regional economic stability and sustainable development, capacity building in macro- and microeconomic management, financial supervision, corporate governance, human resource and sustainable development are most necessary for regional cooperation. Financial cooperation should first help to resume market confidence. This is why monetary and financial cooperation started from the easier bilateral swap arrangements. In order to achieve more balanced development in the region, more sub-regional developments, like the Great Mekong River sub-regional project (GMS), should be promoted.

The multi-layered model which refers mostly to trade and investment liberalization, is called a model of "competitive regional liberalization and cooperation".[10] We have already seen examples, like AFTA, Japan-Singapore Close Economic Partnership (JSCEP) and China–ASEAN FTA (still under negotiation). More such bilateral or sub-grouping trade and investments may be

---

[10] Naoko Munakata, Seize the moment for East Asian Economic Integration. Center for Strategic and International Studies, *PacNet Newsletter*, February 2002. www.brook.edu.

concluded not just intra-region, but also inter-region. As a first step, these rule-based arrangements will help to set up a legal foundation for regional institution-building and also to benefit developing economies in the process of participating in regional integration.

East Asian cooperation and integration is a comprehensive process. Although few had envisaged a regional identity as the final goal, the gradual institution-building is necessary. The cooperation process started from economic need. Economic cooperation is based on immediate demand (the financial crisis) and the foundation of high-level interdependence created by the market. In the political and security areas, both demand and the foundation seem very weak. Nevertheless, separating the economic cooperation process from the political and security process does not mean that the latter is not important and necessary. It is necessary that each be achieved by different ways and at different speeds: while economic cooperation and integration may move faster toward a higher level, the political and security process may move slower and at a lower level. However, it should be recognized that regional cooperation and integration in East Asia needs political trust and security dialogue and arrangement.

There is a long way to go before the different arrangements can be unified into an integrated framework or a regional institution. But efforts should be made in this direction during the process.

IV. Designing Stages and Approaches

While European countries had a clear political goal when they launched their regional cooperation movement in the early 1950s, the countries of East Asia did not when they started their dialogue for cooperation in the late 1990s. Given its multi-layered approach, it is only reasonable for East Asian countries to consolidate all different processes and integrate these gradually into a regional identity. In order to realize the East Asian identity, the whole movement may be represented by the following design based on different processes:

1. A free trade and investment area.

   East Asian market liberalization used to be based mostly on the multilateral approach since real regional trade arrangements (RTA, bilateral or group) did not take place until the late 1990s. ASEAN was formed in 1967 and AFTA was launched in 1992. Japan and ROK began to approach RTA from 1999 when they proposed a bilateral FTA. Since then, several other initiatives have been made between Japan–Singapore, China–ASEAN and Japan–ASEAN. Only Japan and Singapore have concluded their negotiation and signed an agreement for closer economic partnership (CEP) in early 2002. China and ASEAN are still preparing for their negotiation, which is expected to be concluded in 2003. Japan and ROK may still need some time before they can finalize their negotiation by overcoming "the agriculture syndrome". The ROK–ASEAN FTA may be initiated by ROK in 2003 after the election. What is left is China–Japan, China–ROK or China–Japan–ROK. Three countries are now conducting their joint research on trade and investment barriers. A package of trade and investment facilitation arrangements, rather than a FTA, may be recommended. It should be a valuable contribution if three countries could sign such an agreement first.[11]

   With the progress of these multi-layered arrangements, it is reasonable to expect a "convergent process", either by converging three "ASEAN+1 FTAs", or by launching a new EAFTA or East Asian closer economic partnership (EACEP). The research work for an EAFTA or EACEP should start early and

---

[11] Changjie Lee argued that "a Northeast Asia FTA between China, Japan and Korea could be realized before an East Asia FTA". Paper presented at the conference on Asian Economic Integration, organized by Research Institute of Economy, Trade and Industry, Tokyo, Japan, April 22-23, 2002, p. 17.

hopefully, the negotiation can be concluded by 2010 with implementation and transition of 5–10 years, i.e. by 2015 for most members, and by 2020 for less developed economies.[12] This EAFTA or EACEP will be a major component of an East Asian identity.[13]

2. Financial cooperation and monetary integration.

Japan took the lead to promote financial cooperation in the East Asian region by proposing the Asian Monetary Fund (AMF) in 1997 during the Asian financial crisis. But real progress was made only in 2000 when APT financial ministers proposed the CMI, which was quickly confirmed by APT leaders. CMI is considered as a big step in promoting East Asian financial cooperation though it is based on bilateral swap arrangements and the sum of committed funds is not large. The potential significance of these bilateral swaps is the pooling of regional financial resources to be operated under the APT framework in the future. This is helpful to recovering market confidence and attracting capital flow into the region. However, the question is how to link all these bilateral swaps together under a regional network and whether it is necessary to turn the committed swap funds into a regional fund and managed by a regional institution.

It is desirable that formal linkages or institutional frameworks be created for all bilateral swaps after the conclusion of negotiations. An East Asian financial facility may be needed for managing regional swaps, regional financial surveillance and early warning system. This work could be finished by 2005.

This is an easy and effective way to integrate regional financial and monetary arrangements. This approach may differ from a monetary fund. It is modelled on a concept of sharing

---

[12] As proposed in the EAVG report, the establishment of EAFTA will be well ahead of APEC's Borgor goal, i.e. 2020, which will surely be beneficial to realize it.

[13] EAFTA will be comprehensive, including trade, investment and service. An EACEP will certainly be more desirable.

resources and cooperative management. In the future, based on the real desire, it may be necessary to enlarge the size of swaps commitments, to grow the pooling fund. East Asian economies have the world's largest foreign exchange reserves. It is desirable that the pooling of a certain proportion of the foreign exchange reserves be considered as a regional conservative reserve facility in addition to the swaps. Measures should be taken to encourage reserves to be recycled within the East Asian region.

A more important development for financial cooperation is to strengthen cooperation on macroeconomic policy, financial market regulation and financial surveillance.

This needs regional institution-building and capacity-building by the individual country. Regional financial cooperation requires high-level policy coordination, as well as timely information exchange and exposure.

As a matter of fact, it is very important in regional financial cooperation, to develop a good financial system in each country (especially for developing economies) and a well-functioning regional network for finance and payment.

As for monetary cooperation, in order to avoid dramatic fluctuation of exchange rates, it is necessary to encourage each economy to move to a stable floating system weighted on a basket of currencies, rather than to create a collective floating system in the region since the latter needs very high-level policy integration. This can provide an alternative model for regional monetary cooperation by avoiding a controversial monetary fund or a regional monetary regime. This model may be developed at a faster speed than EAFTA or EACEP, for example, to be completed by 2010.

East Asia should develop its own model of monetary and financial cooperation. A regional common currency and/or a regional monetary authority seem very far-off.

3. Political and security cooperation.

East Asia needs political and security cooperation which is an integral part of regional convergence. Considering the diversity and complexity of regional politics and security, this process should be done cautiously and gradually.

Political cooperation may start in the following areas:

(1) Establishing a system (for example, hotlines) for emergency consultation among the leaders.
(2) Consolidation and transparency of legal as well as regulation systems.
(3) Institutionalizing parliament cooperation.

Security cooperation may start in the following areas:

(1) Strengthening military exchanges.
(2) Joint operation and institutional arrangements in non-traditional security areas.
(3) Initiating Defense Ministers' meeting.
(4) Developing conflict and crisis-prevention mechanism.

Political and security cooperation are also multi-layered approaches. The regional efforts will not necessarily reject other existing or future bilateral or group-based arrangements. For example, in security cooperation, instead of forming a common regional policy, institutional arrangements could be developed to parallel other developments both intra- and inter-region. A council (starting from a forum) for consolidating East Asian security concerns may be necessary in the mid-term.

Political and security cooperation should follow an "easy-first approach". In this regard, non-traditional security cooperation should move first and faster.

4. The Organization for East Asian Cooperation.

Institution-building is crucial for the process of East Asian cooperation. Although institution-building starts from a low level and on a multi-layered structure, progress must be achieved in developing a convergent institution for East Asia. A important step is to consider moving from the APT structure to a regional organization, i.e. Organization of East Asian

Cooperation (OEAC). OEAC will have a secretariat and functional committees. It will not only continue current activities, but also develop new functions. The annual leaders' meeting will, of course, be a core activity. As a preparatory process in moving the APT to the OEAC, a secretariat for APT may be necessary soon.

OEAC will not replace or unify other multi-layered arrangements in the region in the near future. However, efforts should be made to develop frameworks and institutions on the regional level, such as EAFTA, financial arrangements and sub-regional development projects. Political and security cooperation should also be finally integrated into OEAC. OEAC's major role is organizing and coordinating, rather than mandating, regional affairs. OEAC should extend its membership to all East Asian countries finally.

There is a long way to go before East Asia is fully integrated. But efforts must be made from the beginning in developing an integrated framework. As a Chinese saying puts it, "A successful start is half the work done."

V. Role of China–ASEAN FTA Initiative

In 2001 at their meeting in Brunei,.the leaders of China and ASEAN agreed to establish a free trade area (FTA) within 10 years. Preparation for the formal negotiation of the agreement is proceeding smoothly.

The question has often been raised: Why did China take the initiative? The answer lies in the potential gains. The establishment of a FTA between China and ASEAN will create an economic region with huge benefits.[14] Trade and investment will increase

---

[14] According to the simulation conducted by the ASEAN Secretariat, a China–ASEAN FTA will increase ASEAN's export to China by 48% and China's export to ASEAN by 55.1%. It will increase China's GDP by 0.3 percent or by US$2.2 billion in absolute terms, ASEAN's GDP by 0.9 percent or by US$5.4 billion. See *Forging closer ASEAN–China economic relations in the twenty-first century*, a report by ASEAN-China Expert Group on Economic Cooperation, 2001.

within the region, and the region itself will become more attractive to other investors. A FTA will provide new impetus to future economic dynamism.

Both China and ASEAN are confident in making a FTA since their economic levels are similar and economic structures highly complimentary. Ten years would give them flexibility to adjust and to implement the agreement.

The significance of the China–ASEAN FTA goes beyond economic benefits. It will bring the two sides closer in their rules and standards. Also, the economic integration will contribute immensely to peace and stability between China and ASEAN and the East Asian region.

What is its impact on East Asian regional cooperation as a whole?[15] From a positive perspective, it may press Japan and ROK to formulate a free trade arrangement with ASEAN and encourage China, Japan and ROK to facilitate closer economic arrangement (for example, an early agreement for trade and investment facilitation). Therefore, the China–ASEAN FTA can be considered as a positive step for the process of East Asian cooperation.

But East Asian cooperation and integration will come up against a variety of difficulties and setbacks.

Japan, as the second largest economy in the world and the largest in the East Asian region? plays a key role in the process of East Asian cooperation. Japan has participated in the APT process and successfully signed a FTA with Singapore. However, Japan has not played a leading role yet in the process of East Asian cooperation and integration for the following reasons:

(1) The current economic difficulty, which discourages the government from making any bold commitment.

---

[15] It has been questioned that the "challenge is to work out how they fit together in the regionalism portfolio". Christopher Findlay and Mari Pangestu: Regional trade arrangements in East Asia: Where are they taking us? Paper presented at PECC Trade Policy Forum Symposium, June 12–13, 2001, Bangkok, Thailand, p. 20.

(2) The American-centered relationship, which significantly affects Japan's attitude to and interests in taking the lead in East Asian integration.
(3) A protective agriculture sector prevents the government from promoting or even participating in comprehensive regional liberation arrangements.

Japan does not seem ready to make East Asian regionalism its priority.[16] Japan is still swaying between America and East Asia and struggling with domestic restructuring without fundamental change of its protective agricultural sector. Given a rising China, Japan is under pressure to respond to China's move or initiate its own action. A passive approach restrains Japan's positive role as a key factor in promoting regional cooperation and integration.

Japan has significant economic, political and security interests in East Asian which are best served by regional cooperation and integration. It is important for Japan to overcome the "American syndrome" as well as the "China syndrome". Of course, other countries should encourage and support Japan's active participation and leading role in some areas.

Great concern has been raised on the attitudes and roles of China and Japan in the process of East Asian cooperation. It is obvious that the East Asian cooperation process cannot proceed smoothly without the active participation and cooperation of the two countries. Both have already built up significant economic interests through trade and investment. But real trust has not been created due to major differences in political understanding and security concerns. The two still treat each other as rivals, rather than close partners.

---

[16] Junichiro Koizumi Prime Minister of Japan talked about the creation of a community that "acts together and advances together", "to make the best use of the framework of ASEAN+3" when he visited Singapore on 14 January 2002, but with few accountable measures. See "Japan and ASEAN in East Asia — a sincere and open partnership", speech by Koizumi in Singapore.

As a matter of fact, the process of East Asian cooperation and integration is an important mechanism for both countries to create common interests and build up trust. China should accept and support Japan's leading role in areas where Japan has the advantage, and vice versa. China should consider Japan's giant economic strength as a valuable regional wealth, and Japan should treat a rising China and its active role in the region positively. In so doing, China and Japan can become partners bilaterally and in regional affairs. A positive trend has been witnessed, for example, in promoting of trilateral dialogue (China, Japan and ROK), swap arrangements, and sub-regional development, but this is insufficient.

It is important to create security convergence for East Asia if the region is to become integrated. Considering the regional divide in traditional security, China has proposed to start the cooperation first in the non-traditional security field. To do this, the areas and priorities of non-traditional security must first be identified, before consolidated policy, and joint action and operation can be developed.

China and ASEAN has moved in a right direction by initiating a "Code of Conduct" aiming at reducing tension and securing stability in the dispute over the South China Sea. The Shanghai Organization of Cooperation has set a good example in the cooperation of traditional security by building trust through joint-military reduction along the border areas. While, non-traditional security cooperation should start first, this does not mean that no effort should be made for traditional security. Here, East Asia may start with regional military exchange program and security dialogue for defense ministers. East Asia should develop its own security arrangement. A rational "Pacific Security Arrangement" should be based on the cooperation between East Asia and North America.[17]

---

[17] US–Japan military alliance based on bilateral relationship may continue to exist if both sides consider it necessary. This does not conflict with the East Asian security arrangement.

The differences in economic development levels are very large in East Asia. One of the major functions for East Asian cooperation and integration is to reduce the development gap, i.e. helping the less developed countries to catch up. There are several ways to do this — such as providing preferential treatment for less developed economies in their participation in regional free trade and investment arrangement, and strengthening cooperation on sub-regional economic development projects, like the GMS. In order to develop the regional capacity, a regional development fund would be necessary under OEAC in the future. At the same time, it is necessary to make capacity-building for the less developed countries a major priority.

It is vital to secure the participation of the less developed countries to benefit the process of regional cooperation and integration.

The train of East Asian cooperation and integration has started with no clear final destination yet. The real value is the journey. However, the train needs to be fueled along the way and the final goal needs to be identified through consensus-building.

CHAPTER FIVE

Northeast Asian Community: Is it Possible to Turn Vision into Reality?[1]

Introduction

Community-building has been proposed as a goal for Northeast Asian cooperation. What does "community-building" mean? It is agreed that due to the great diversity of the Northeast Asian region, this community is not a European-type regional organization with the power of managing regional affairs. The aim of the Northeast Asian community-building is to create an environment for living together peacefully and for realizing prosperity through cooperation. Community-building can be defined as a value for living together and also as the spirit for cooperation.

Economically, a community will make the regional economies highly integrated and enable them to share interests for common prosperity. Intra-regional trade and investment flow would be well developed through liberalization and cooperation arrangements. The purpose of the Northeast Asian community is not to establish a super-regional organization, but to conduct regional economic activities according to agreed rules and standards. If necessary, the

---

[1] This paper was written for the Jeju Peace Conference held at Jeju, ROK, 10–11 June 2005.

regional institutions can be used for consultation and coordination.[2] The regional community should develop a spirit of cooperation aiming at solving common issues together, like the environment, transportation, energy etc. and helping the less developed economies to catch up.

Politically, a community will make the region stable and build trust through cooperation. Northeast Asia shares history and culture, but also grievances and even conflicts. Based on the spirit of community, countries in the region should develop a good-neighbor policy and solve their differences through consultation and cooperation. Diversity is a reality in the region. Differences should not be the reason for leaving out any member in the regional community. Political respect and tolerance should be a cultural norm for Northeast Asia. Mass media and new media should help to create this shared culture and value. The cooperation of the three major countries, i.e. China, the Republic of Korea (ROK) and Japan is essential in leading the region towards becoming a community. These leaders should establish a formal mechanism both for normal exchanges and emergency meetings.

In the aspect of security, a community should realize the lasting peace of the region. Northeast Asia is still divided by the division of the Korean Peninsula and its security architecture. Community-building should help to resolve the confrontation on the Korean Peninsula and develop a integrated security framework for all members, based on the existing "Six Party Talks" if it can move forward with success. A community should also develop the means for solving remaining or emerging problems through consultation and cooperation.

The Northeast Asian community should be represented by a comprehensive cooperation framework combining multi-layered mechanisms supporting formal agreements, cooperation programs both at central and local government levels, exchanges of civil

---

[2] Chang Jae Lee (2004). Rational for institutionalizing Northeast Asian economic cooperation and some possible options. In *Strengthening Economic Cooperation in Northeast Asia.* Yoon Hyung Kim and Chang Jae Lee (eds.). Seoul: KIEP, p. 23.

societies, as well as some possible institutional establishment. The region should not be governed by an integrated regional organization with all countries participating.[3]

Skepticism prevails over Northeast Asian community-building since it faces so many obstacles. The first thing for community-building is to cultivate a spirit of respect and trust, not just among governments, but also among the people in their respective societies. Community-building is a process that should gradually deepen and expand. Effort must be put in to realize the vision for our future.

I. Foundation: Economic Integration

The three economies of China, Japan and ROK account for the vast majority of the Northeast Asian regional economy. Their economies have increasingly become integrated. This has been reflected by the fast increase of trade and other economic exchanges between the three bilaterally i.e. between China–Japan, China–ROK and ROK–Japan (Table 1).

Importantly, the integration is created by FDI-led intra-trade and related-service activities. FDI flow becomes a focal factor in

Table 1: Trade relations between China, ROK and Japan (in billion US dollars, export and import).

	China–Japan	China–Korea	Korea–Japan
2000	83.1	34.5	52.3
2001	87.8	35.9	43.1
2002	101.9	44.1	44.0
2004	167.9	90.1	53.6*

* For 2003.
Source: China Statistics, JETRO, Statistics and Surveys.

---

[3] It is difficult to build up a regional organization with functions to govern regional affairs. See Zhang Yunling (ed.). *Northeast Asian Economic Cooperation.* World Affairs Publisher, 2004, Beijing, p. 3.

making the three economies more and more integrated since increasing share of trade between them are investment-related. For example, for about 40 percent of Japanese and Korean companies investing in China, their intra-firm trade share is as high as 75 percent; almost half of Japanese companies investing in China export over 75 percent of their products to Japan.[4] Although FDI flows are currently mainly from Japan and ROK to China, economic integration finds its rationale through efficient restructuring of the manufacturing industries. This intra-industrial division of production and services has helped to build up a network which made the three economies highly interdependent and beneficial to one an other. The restructuring of manufacturing industries among the three countries have created new businesses in services, like finance, transportation, logistics, and has also encouraged more and more movement of human resources between them. Projecting from China's economic progress, capital flow from China to Japan and ROK will also increase which will help to create a more balanced structure for economic integration.

However, this economic integration has been driven mostly by market forces based on companies' business strategies to maximize profit. It has been argued that market-driven restructuring by companies would hurt the home economy by creating the "hollowing out" effect. But the facts show that running manufacturing and service industries based on comparative advantages has created significant benefits to all sides, even to FDI home countries due to their rational restructuring. China has benefited largely from receiving FDIs from ROK and Japan that has helped it to develop its modern manufacturing industries and build up competitive capacity both for export and the domestic market. At the same time, both ROK and Japan have benefited from timely restructuring of their economies to help improve their competitiveness.

---

[4] Zhang Qi, Major impediments to intra-regional investment between China, Japan and Korea. Paper presented at Symposium on Strengthening Economic Cooperation in Northeast Asia, Beijing, 29 September 2002.

This complimentary structure of economic linkages among the three economies will continue into the future.

Economic integration calls for institutional transparency and stability, market liberalization and close macroeconomic coordination. Without institutional arrangements, business transactions may be blocked by all kinds of tariff and non-tariff barriers. As a matter of fact, non-tariff restrictions still largely exist between China, ROK and Japan.

Furthermore, the participation of other economies in the entire Northeast Asian region should be encouraged. Mongolia, Russia, and the Democratic People's Republic of Korea (DPRK) belong to the region. Trade exchanges and investment flows, as well as network building, should be gradually extended to these economies.

It is important to keep the Northeast Asian cooperation network under a two-track structure: one is China, ROK and Japan (also under the framework of "10+3"), another track is for the other members in the region, i.e. Mongolia, Russia and DPRK. The second track will support selected projects. It is valuable if China, ROK and Japan could set up a summit meeting in the future and invite the other Northeast Asian leaders to attend.[5]

II. Progress of Economic Cooperation

Economic integration requires economic cooperation. Northeast Asian economic cooperation has been developed in a multi-layered structure in institutional and non-institutional ways.

On an institutional level, the FTA is the most important development. ROK and Japan has already signed their investment agreement and started their FTA negotiation from 2003 and they have tried hard to conclude it by the end of 2005. China and ROK

---

[5] The cooperation mechanism for the security of the Northeast Asian region should also be extended to non-regional members, especially the US, due to the complex nature. A security framework for the region may be based on the current Six-Party Talks.

will start their FTA feasibility study in 2005 and negotiation may start from 2006. Due to the difficulty on ROK side (opening the agriculture market), this process may be a very hard one. China and Japan have not prepared to start their FTA process yet. Japan has originally called for a bilateral investment agreement, but China hopes to negotiate a close economic partnership agreement covering trade, investment and service. The joint study group for a trilateral FTA, submitted to the Trilateral Summit Meeting in 2003 a report and policy proposal on strengthening trilateral cooperation. It evaluated the economic effects of a trilateral free trade agreement, and concluded that it would bring about substantial macroeconomic effects favorable to the three countries. A joint study on the possible modality of trilateral investment arrangements was conducted, with the common understanding that the promotion of trilateral investment would increase dynamism of the three countries' domestic economies and strengthen trilateral economic cooperation. It suggested that a legal framework should be explored concerning the trilateral investment. But considering the differences of the policy priorities and interests, the trilateral FTA for China, ROK and Japan does not seem to be on the immediate agenda though China has called for an early start.[6]

An important step of progress is the joint declaration on promotion of tripartite cooperation among the three countries in Bali, Indonesia on 7 October 2003 during the leaders' meeting between China, Japan and Korea. As stated in the declaration, with geographical proximity, economic complementarity, growing economic cooperation and increasing people-to-people exchanges, the three countries have become important economic and trade partners to one another, and have continuously strengthened their

---

[6] Michael G. Plummer argued that rising levels of inter-regional trade and investment flows in Northeast Asia derive mainly from interaction with China, rather than between Japan and South Korea. He suggested that "if the flag is to follow trade, the agreement should be three-way". See Yoon Hyung Kim and Chang Jae Lee (eds.) (2004). *Strengthening Economic Cooperation in Northeast Asia*. Seoul: KIEP, p. 174.

coordination and cooperation in regional and international affairs. The cooperation among the three countries demonstrates the gratifying momentum for the development of their relations.[7]

The leaders of the three countries have held regular informal meetings since 1999. Departments of various portfolios have established mechanisms for meetings at the ministerial, senior official and working levels. The areas of cooperation include trade and investment facilitation measures ranging from customs, transportation and quality supervision, inspection and quarantine.[8] For example, bilateral meetings on customs have exchanged views on measures for swift customs clearance to facilitate trade. The customs mutual assistance agreement (CMAA) between China and ROK is already in place, a ROK–Japan CMAA will soon be ready and a China–Japan CMAA is now under negotiation. In the transportation area, the Northeast Asia Port Directors-General Meetings have been held since September 2000. Joint studies are conducted on promotion of cruising, investment and free-trade zones and new design of port facilities. In the information and communications technology area, the trilateral ICT Ministers' Meetings had been formalized and closer trilateral cooperation and the framework of an "East Asia (CJK) ICT Summit" were agreed on. Working groups have met for cooperation in six areas (the next generation Internet (IPv6), 3G and next generation mobile communications, network and information security, telecommunication service policies, digital TV and broadcasting, open source software).

Environmental cooperation has also achieved progress: a comprehensive sub-regional environmental cooperation mechanism in

---

[7] Declaration on Promotion of Tripartite Cooperation among Three Countries, Bali, Indonesia on 7 October 2003.

[8] The leaders agreed in the Joint Declaration on promotion of cooperation in 14 areas including economy and trade, culture, people-to-people exchanges, and politics and security, as well as the establishment of the Three-Party Committee which is headed by the foreign ministers of the three countries to study, plan, coordinate and monitor the cooperation activities. See Joint Declaration on the Promotion of Tripartite Cooperation, Trilateral Summit, 2003.

Northeast Asia, and the monitoring and early warning network system for dust and sand storms, the Acid Deposition Monitoring Network in East Asia, the Northwest Pacific Action Plan for the protection of the regional marine and coastal environment, the Northeast Asia Sub-regional Program for Environmental Cooperation. The "Partnerships in Environmental Management for the Seas of East Asia" has provided the framework for cooperation in sustainable development of the seas.

Energy cooperation is considered as one of the most important areas that Northeast Asian countries should cooperate on both for energy consumption and energy supply. China, ROK and Japan are Asia's three largest energy-consuming countries. Their three energy ministers met in 2004 and agreed to further deepen their cooperation and partnership. However, their competition for energy supply security, have stood in the way. An energy community can only be built up by a cooperative spirit and cooperative policies for both major energy consumers and suppliers. In reality, neither the three major energy-consuming countries, nor key energy-supplying countries have taken real action in moving towards becoming an energy community.

Cooperation in IT among the three countries has been developing through both corporate initiatives and governmental efforts. The Northeast Asian IT R&D standard and network (new generation internet, phone system etc.) is being developed. It is proposed that an IT common market should first be developed by China, ROK and Japan which forms an important foundation for the Northeast Asian FTA.[9]

Cooperation for promoting tourism in the Northeast Asian region has been given special attention in recent years. In order to stimulate tourism demand, China, ROK and Japan tourism authorities have launched joint tourism promotion programs linking the

---

[9] Kim Yong Ho (2005). New pattern of economic cooperation in Northeast Asia and the cooperation among Korea, China and Japan. *Journal of Northeast Asia Studies*, 1, Tianjin, China, p. 8.

three countries as a single destination. Trilateral exchanges of tourism have become more active with this new initiative.

Cooperation in other areas like education, cultural exchange, etc., has also been developed.

Sub-regional cooperation also exist, like the Tumen River development program, China–Russia border close economic ties, new emerging ROK–DPRK Kaisen industrial development zone etc. Cooperation between the local cities and communities on port linkage, resource development, urban management etc. has been developed more actively than by the central governments. The community-building in the region usually finds its momentum in this "grass root" movement.

The development of cooperation currently among China, ROK and Japan serves as a gradual process for community-building in the Northeast Asian region. However, the progress is too slow and limited for high-level economic integration and interdependence of the three countries. The trilateral cooperation is reflected more by meetings or forums. In the key areas, like macroeconomic coordination, the trilateral FTA, the energy community etc. real institution-building and joint actions are far from satisfactory.

III. East Asian Cooperation Context

Northeast Asian cooperation is an integral part of the East Asian cooperation process. The East Asian cooperation process, currently in the form of "10+3", formally started after the 1997 financial crisis. Notable achievements have already been made: an institutional framework for regional cooperation through annual leaders' meetings, ministers' meetings (currently 10 areas) and senior officials' meetings; real progress in financial cooperation through the Chiang Mai Initiative, the preferential trade arrangements (PTA), like AFTA, China–ASEAN FTA, Japan–Singapore closer economic partnership agreement (JSCEP) and on going Japan–ASEAN, ROK–ASEAN FTA negotiations, as well as sub-regional development projects, like the Great Mekong Development Project (GMS).

The foundation of East Asian cooperation rests on the increasing economic convergence of the region, in which Northeast Asian economies have played the key role. Until the 1997 financial crisis, the regional economy did well. The crisis showed the vulnerability of East Asian market-based integration. East Asian cooperation will help to improve the conditions for regional economic growth and stability.

The goal of East Asian cooperation remained unclear when the East Asia Summit was held in 2005. Although there is no consensus yet the movement towards regional cooperation will not stop. East Asian countries try to adopt a pragmatic approach. A multi-layered model catering mostly to trade and investment liberalization fits the regional reality. Importantly, by concluding the negotiated agreements, it helps to follow the rules and standards for regional economic activities which constitutes the legal foundation for regional institution-building.

East Asian cooperation and integration is a comprehensive process. Although it is difficult to envisage a regional identity like the EU as the final goal, gradual institution-building seems inevitable. By starting with a multi-layered process, it is necessary for East Asian countries to consolidate all the different processes before integrating into a single regional arrangement.

Northeast Asia should play an active role in supporting and promoting East Asian community-building due to its weight in the region. While making more efforts to move its own regional cooperation process, it should show its key role in moving the East Asian process faster. Although ASEAN will continue to play a special role in leading East Asian community-building, the key role of China, ROK and Japan should be designated. It is important for the three countries to jointly move the Northeast Asian FTA faster, or to push the East Asian FTA (EAFTA) based on three "10+1" FTAs (China–ASEAN, Japan–ASEAN and ROK–ASEAN). They should also play a significant role in helping the less developed countries in East Asia to improve their economies and enhance their capacity to meet the challenges from market liberalization.

The East Asian cooperation process helps to facilitate Northeast Asian cooperation. It is the "10+3" process that has helped to bring the three Northeast Asian leaders together and set the course for a formalized annual leaders' meeting and other governmental cooperation mechanisms. In this aspect, East Asian cooperation serves to bind the Northeast Asian countries together and presses them to move faster.

IV. Vulnerable Political Trust

Community-building needs political trust and cooperation among the countries in the region. Due to historical grievances as well as current differences, the Northeast East Asian region needs political reconciliation based on normalized and improved bilateral relations. While the political reconciliation process has started, it has a long way to go.

China, ROK and Japan started their high-level political dialogue under the framework of "10+3" from 2000. This has led to trilateral economic cooperation and helped to improve political relations by enhancing them understanding and trust among. However, the trilateral cooperation still needs sound bilateral relations. Trust-building cannot be done without consolidating the understanding of the three countries' historical ties. Japan's tendency to mislead on Northeast Asian historical issues is a sticking point with China and ROK. This makes the political foundation for trilateral cooperation very vulnerable.

To overcome this dilemma, Japan should do more in trusting the other Northeast Asian countries by stopping any top leader to visit Yasukuni Shrine again and teaching the real facts of history to its people. China and ROK should also take more forward-looking measures in helping their people move beyond past injustices. Government officials have great responsibility to reduce rather than increase hostility between peoples.

Trust between China and Japan is crucial for Northeast Asian community-building. In facing China's quick rise, Japan seems to consider it as detrimental to its interests. This has constrained the Japanese government from making bold overtures towards China, and reflects a lack of strategic vision.[10] On the Chinese side, both Japan's sincerity in addressing its past militarisms and its current intentions towards China remain questions.[11] Anti-Japanese feelings have hardened among young Chinese.

Likewise with ROK-Japan relations. Despite efforts at improving bilateral relations by the two governments, the newly emerging conflict on historical issue and dispute on the island have deteriorated the people's trust.

Emerging nationalism is considered to be behind the problem. As a leading Japanese columnist pointed out, "Such hostile attitudes towards one another, if unchecked, could have disastrous effect."[12] What can be done? The first thing is to improve bilateral relations through new efforts. As history comprises specific issues that cannot be easily overcome, the Japanese government should take real action to address the major concerns raised by its neighbours. Current territorial disputes and the East Sea "exclusive economic zone" (EEZ) issue should be handled through cooperation. The parties concerned should prepare together for negotiation on disputed islands and sea borders. As a trilateral mechanism exists for high-level dialogue and cooperation, these issues should be discussed during the summit. This requires strengthening of the role of the summit. Furthermore, government to government dialogues alone are not enough. People to people exchanges and the participation of NGOs should be encouraged. Northeast Asia needs more regional-based civilian cooperative institutions.

---

[10] Takahara Akio (2004). Japan's Political Response to the Rise of China. In *The Rise of China and a Changing East Asian Order*, Kokubun Ryosei and Wang Jisi (eds.). Tokyo: JCIE, p. 170.

[11] Xu Jian, a Chinese scholar argued that compared with other powers, Japan seems to have even more reservations over the rapid development of China. Paper presented at The International Symposium on Peace and Prosperity in Northeast Asia, 13 January 2005, Seoul: Conference papers, p. 30.

[12] See Yoichi Funabashi, source same as footnote 7, p. 41.

While community-building in Northeast Asia needs all bilateral relations improved, the process itself should significantly help to enhance such relations. A strong political back up for economic cooperation between the three countries should become a core institution to enable other members in Northeast Asia to join in the community-building. However, its foundation is currently, too weak.

Security also needs to be handled well for Northeast Asian community-building. There are two general security challenges: one is the divided security structure, i.e. US military alliance and another is the division and confrontation on the Korean Peninsula. This existing division is a result of the Cold War which should not be the only security arrangement. The division of the Korean Peninsula may be the excuse for its maintenance, but is not helpful for solving the Korean conflict. The Six Party Talks are on working the nuclear managing of DPRK ambitions. But it is clear that the nuclear issue cannot be solved independently without other comprehensive arrangements since it has evolved from a complex relationship that spans decades. It would be desirable if the Six Party Talks could be part of a Northeast Asian security framework in the future. US participation of the new Northeast security framework is necessary since it is a key factor to all security matters.[13] However, the real test for the Northeast Asian security framework is whether it can be changed from being confrontational to cooperative, i.e. a new cooperative security arrangement. At the same time, this should not replace cooperation among the three countries, either on the bilateral or trilateral level.

Due to the complexity of the Northeast Asia political and security situation, regional cooperation is focused on the economy and community-building. But the Northeast Asian community needs a broad foundation of economic, political, and security mechanisms though the economic mechanism should and could go faster than the others.

---

[13] Kent Calder and Min Ye (2004). Regionalism and Critical Junctures: Explaining the Organization Gap in Northeast Asia. *Journal of East Asian Studies*, 4, p. 215.

V. China and ROK Working Together

China and ROK are two major players in Northeast Asian community-building as reflected on three levels: their individual position and role in the region; their mutual relationship, and their joint efforts.

China, though still a developing country, with its large size, big population and fast-growing economy is playing a special role not just in contributing to the regional economic dynamism, but also in promoting regional cooperation and helping regional stability. The role of China's market to the region is increasingly important. China's market is the binding factor through trade and FDI flows that bring the Northeast East Asian economies together within a production and business network. China actively promotes and participates in regional cooperation. In 2001, China proposed setting up the economic and trade ministers' meetings; the following year, it proposed a feasibility study on the trilateral FTA of China, ROK and Japan.

In the political and security aspects, China, practises its peace and development long strategy and "good neighbor policy", plays an positive role in reducing regional tension and improve the security environment by initiating and participating in the Six-Party Talks.

ROK, as a member of OECD, is more economically advanced than China. It has competitive advantages in IT and some other areas. ROK becomes an important source for FDI flow to China. Based on its long strategy, it is putting in effort to become the center for Northeast Asian logistics, IT and entertainment industries.

ROK's position is unique in transferring the conflicted Korean Peninsula to a cooperative and finally a united and peaceful place. Its "one Northeast Asia" vision and initiative helps to create a "shared value for trust, mutual interest and living together' which is the foundation for the Northeast Asian community-building.[14]

---

[14] Moon Chung In (2005). Northeast Asian Economic Community and Coping Strategy. *Journal of Northeast Asian Studies*, 1, p. 6.

China–ROK relations have developed in a comprehensive way. Economically, the two countries have established a highly independent structure. China has become the largest export and FDI market for ROK. In 2004, the two-way trade between the two countries exceeded US$90 billion and in 2005 it will surpass US$100 billion. An important change is that trade between the two countries has moved to a high structural level with most of the traffic in capital and high-tech products. FDI from ROK to China has increased rapidly. In 2004, ROK was the largest source among all FDI flows to China, the accumulated investment size reaching US$25.8 billion, the fourth largest FDI by country, only after US, Japan and Singapore. It is estimated that more than 40 percent of ROK companies have investments in China. China has gained significantly from receiving FDI flows and importing IT intermediate products. ROK also has benefited remarkably by investing in China since this helps it to restructure its economy and make it more competitive. The highly complimentary nature of China–ROK economic relations will continue to exist for the future.[15] More importantly, the two economies are integrated China will continue to provide a secure and huge market for ROK. This is a win-win formula, though both sides have to manage to future competitive challenges both from each other and other parties.[16]

An early comprehensive FTA for China and ROK is highly beneficial to both. The two governments are preparing to start the negotiation process. China–ROK FTA will facilitate the process of the China–Japan FTA and, perhaps, the trilateral FTA.

The trust between China and ROK must be enhanced to develop a comprehensive cooperative partnership. Differences

---

[15] China's investment in ROK will increase along with its economic upgrading. China may become the largest investor in ROK in the coming future. Cao Shigong (2005). An Evaluation on the Economic Relations between China and Korea. *Northeast Asian Studies*, 1, p. 11.

[16] It has been suggested that Korea should take China's challenge as a catalyst for its industrial upgrading and domestic reforms, rather than treating it as a threat. Nam Young-Sook (2004). China's Indusrial Rise and the Challenges Facing Korea. *East Asian Review*, 16(2), p. 64.

should be solved through consultation and cooperation. Thus, China and ROK should cooperate more broadly than just the economic area. The two countries share a common interest in keeping peace based on gradual transition of the Korean Peninsula relations. They play a key role together in engaging PDRK and integrating it into regional community-building.

China-ROK cooperation will be helpful for the China–Japan relationship which is going through a rough path.[17] In order to build the Northeast Asian community, the three countries must first improve their bilateral relations. China and ROK should take the lead in this direction.

The Northeast Asian community is a vision that needs to be realized both in spirit and with real actions.

---

[17] Jong-Pyo Hong. Regional integration in Northeast Asia: Approaches to Integration among China, Korea and Japan. KIEP, *CHAEC Research Series*, 4(4), p. 18.

CHAPTER SIX

The Development of East Asian FTA[1]

Introduction

Regional trade arrangements (RTAs) have become a very prominent feature of the multilateral trading system and an important trade policy instrument for WTO members. The proliferation of RTAs may be the result of many factors from the economic to the political. They may be as an integrated part of regional movement towards integration and cooperation; as a supplement of multilateral arrangements, i.e. a "WTO plus" formula (faster, or beyond); as an alternative approach when the multilateral negotiation has stalled; as a regional response to globalization; as a policy option to facilitate domestic reform and as a political motivation for closer relations between the related parties. The major component of a RTA is negotiating a free trade agreement (FTA). Compared with multilateral arrangement, FTA has broader coverage although the major content of an FTA is the liberalization and facilitation of trade and investment.[2]

---

[1] This paper is part of the research report written for the workshop organized by ADB Institute on "Multilateralising Asian Regionalism", on 18–19 September 2008, Tokyo. Thanks to Dr. Shen Minghui who helped to collect the related materials.

[2] Roberto V. Fiorentino, Lius Verdeja, Christelle Toqueboeuf (2006). The Changing Landscape of Regional Trade Agreements: 2006 Update. *WTO Discussion Paper*, No. 12, p. 1.

The East Asian region is witnessing multi-layered FTAs. Pioneered by ASEAN in 1992 when it initiated ASEAN FTA (AFTA) and encouraged by "ASEAN+1" FTAs, more and more economies are now involved with RTAs. Due to the different background and condition, each FTA has its own character although all of them are committed to be consistent with WTO. The FTA partners can benefit from market liberalization, trade and investment facilitation in addition to economic cooperation provided by the agreements. However, the question has also been raised on the possible negative impacts of FTAs because of the complexity of different regulations and the "noodle bowl" effect of deriving from the different rules of origin (ROO).

Recognizing the current status of FTAs, the business community in East Asia has warned that the proliferation of FTAs have created new barriers and raised the cost of their business in the region. The leaders in East Asia have instructed the track II study (academic study) on the problems of FTAs and feasibility of an integrated East Asian FTA. East Asian economies are highly integrated and dependent on each other. Based on the high level of FDI flows, intra-regional trade and production network, East Asia will have to move forward from current multi-layered FTAs to wider regional FTA.

I. Current Status of FTAs in East Asia

1. *FTA proliferation in East Asia*

East Asian economies have benefited from the continuous progress of multilateralism in the post Second World War era with the adoption of the export-led economic growth model. In the wave of emerging regionalism in the world, East Asia economies are also taking actions in establishing RTAs. ASEAN, as an early regional organization, took the lead in forming its FTA. AFTA, initiated in 1992, was clearly inspired by the establishment of the EU Single Market and NAFTA.

In East Asia, ASEAN's role is unique. On the one hand, ASEAN itself seeks to benefit from more FTAs with it as a hub which can create a "hub-spoke" structure in the ASEAN+1 FTAs, while on the other hand, as an integrated regional market, ASEAN becomes attractive to other regional partners leading to outside initiatives for making FTA with it.

China, as an emerging economic power, showed its new interest in formulating FTA for broader market access to both WTO and non-WTO members after its accession to WTO in 2000. China's first FTA initiative is with ASEAN. By forging an FTA, China took ASEAN both as a potential regional market and a close geographical partner. This initiative received positive response from ASEAN since it was considered as an important strategy to engage a rising economic power.

China's FTA initiative with ASEAN aroused others' quick responses, especially from Japan and the Republic of Korea (ROK), which led to three parallel ASEAN+1 FTAs in East Asia. Japan used to stick to multilateralism. It is also interested in RTAs since it is a major player in the East Asian production network. FTAs without the involvement of Japan will surely hurt Japanese companies that have intensive business interests in the region. ROK, as a newly emerging trade and investment player in the region, also quickly followed the trend and began to negotiate FTA with ASEAN.

Actually, in making FTAs, few economies restricted themselves only to East Asia. Each one has selected negotiation partners on a global reach. It is clear that FTA has become a new strategy for East Asian economies. Why has the FTA become so important?

In general, the slow progress of WTO Doha Development Agenda (DDA) negotiation encourages its members to seek more regional efforts. FTA has been used by WTO members as a new instrument to explore both the regional and global markets. In this sense, FTA initiatives by East Asian economies are just one scenario of a global trend.

From a regional perspective, East Asian economies are encouraged to turn to practical bilateral or sub-regional approaches by APEC's failure to realize its "Bogor Goal" (free trade and investment in the Asia-Pacific by 2010 for developed members and 2020 for developing members). In 1997, APEC initiated an Early Voluntary Sector Liberalization program (EVSL) by selecting 15 sectors for liberalization. But it failed due to its voluntary approach and the following Asian financial crisis.[3] The slow progress of APEC after the financial crisis in 1997 made its members turn to other FTA agendas.

FTAs in East Asia are also considered as a defensive strategy to globalization and regionalism in other regions. Virtually almost all countries are pursuing FTAs. European integration has deepened greatly since the 1990s — notably through the creation of a single market and the successful launch of the Euro. EU has also admitted transitional economies in Central and Eastern Europe through its further enlargement. In addition to NAFTA, the US has pursued many FTAs around the world. East Asian economies understandably feel compelled to conclude their own agreements with these critical markets.[4] Governments in East Asia fear that unless they develop their own regional trade arrangement, they will be disadvantaged in global competition and multilateral negotiations. In addition, they increasingly realize the importance of uniting themselves to gain bargaining power vis-à-vis the European Union, the United States and other groupings.[5]

The real push is the financial crisis in 1997 that pressed East Asian economies to take a strong regional approach. The crisis helped to create a sense of East Asian economic identity since their economies are highly integrated with each other.[6] This led to the ASEAN+3 dialogue and cooperation framework and other regional cooperation mechanisms.

---

[3] Tubagus Feridhanusetyawan (2005). Preferential Trade Agreements in the Asia-Pacific Region, *IMF Working Paper* 05149, p. 13.

[4] Asian Development Bank (2008). *Emerging Asian Regionalism: A Partnership for Shared Prosperity*, p. 85.

[5] Bergsten, C. F. (2000). Towards a Tripartite World. *The Economist*, pp. 23–25. America's Two-Front Economic Conflict. *Foreign Affairs* (March/April), 2001, pp. 16–28.

[6] Masahiro Kawai (2005). East Asian Economic Regionalism: Progress and Challenges. *Journal of Asian Economics*, 16, p. 16.

FTAs can provide more market access. Compared with the multilateral approach, regional agreement is much more flexible and also faster since problems that would take years to solve in global negotiations can be dealt with more quickly.[7] That is, the small number of parties involved, compared with the WTO, promised greater ease in reaching agreement, and in tailoring agreements to the specific conditions of the members. Many FTAs in the region cover areas not yet covered or covered poorly by WTO arrangement, thus they are packaged as WTO-plus. These include trade liberalization in services and investment, standards, intellectual property rights, capacity-building, economic cooperation and labor mobility etc.[8]

Apart from economic considerations, RTAs are also used to cement the political relationship among the countries involved. For example, ASEAN started as politico-security institution with little attention paid to economic issues. The formation of AFTA in 1992 provided a good platform for ASEAN countries to work more closely. Similarly, the ASEAN–China FTA (ACFTA) was regarded as a political confidence-building process when China emerged as regional power. ASEAN also takes ASEAN+1 FTA initiatives as a strategic design with itself as a hub and also an instrument to its own community-building.

2. FTA development in East Asia

In East Asia, the first FTA proposal was put forward in 1998 for a Japan–ROK FTA, which is now stalled. Later, there were more FTA initiatives, some within East Asia, some with countries in other regions — some concluded, some still under negotiation.

The Japan–Singapore EPA (JSEPA) was considered as a new kind of FTA in the region since it covers more areas than traditional

---

[7] Zhang Yunling (2006). *Designing East Asian FTA: Rationale and Feasibility.* Beijing: Social Sciences Academic Press, pp. 1–2.
[8] Tubagus Feridhanusetyawan (2005). Preferential Trade Agreements in the Asia-Pacific Region. *IMF Working Paper* 05149, p. 14.

liberalization — trade, investment, services, the dispute settlement mechanism, as well as economic and technical cooperation at various functional levels between the two countries. China took the lead in making a large-scale FTA with ASEAN as a group. The China–ASEAN CEP agreement was signed in 2002, which started with an early harvest program focusing on liberalization of major agricultural products and an agricultural cooperation agreement. The ACFTA for trade in goods was signed in November of 2004 and started implementation from July of 2005, and followed with the agreement for trade in services in 2007. In 2003, Japan signed CEP framework agreement with ASEAN and concluded six bilateral FTAs with individual ASEAN members (Singapore, Malaysia, Thailand, Philippines, Brunei and Indonesia). The negotiation of ASEAN–Japan FTA (AJFTA) was concluded in 2008. ROK speeded up her negotiation with ASEAN and ASEAN–ROK FTA (AKFTA) both in goods and in services was concluded in November of 2007.

Including FTAs with other regions, as of June 2008, East Asian economies have concluded 37 FTAs, while 39 are under negotiation and a further 33 proposed. Singapore has concluded the most (15) and has 12 FTAs under negotiation and five proposed, followed by Thailand, China and ROK — each has 24, 23 and 22 FTA initiatives and eight, seven and five under implementation respectively. In general, more developed economies tend to be more active in negotiating FTAs since they have the negotiating capacities. Less developed economies (for example, Cambodia, the Lao People's Democratic Republic, Myanmar) tend to rely more heavily on FTAs based on AFTA and ASEAN+1 instead. Until now, most of the agreements that East Asian economies have concluded or initiated are with non-Asian countries (of total 109 FTAs initiatives, 86 with countries outside East Asia).

As FTAs proliferate, the question of whether greater benefits could be achieved by integrating them naturally arises. The consolidation of East Asian bilateral and regional FTAs has been explored both in the ASEAN+3 (EAFTA) and ASEAN+6 (CEPEA) framework. While no decision has been taken, high interest in such efforts is still there. Also, the initiative in a larger framework, for

Table 1: Free trade agreements in East Asia (ASEAN+3).

Negotiating body	Under Implementation	Signed	Under negotiation	Proposed	Total	Inside EA	Outside EA
ASEAN	3	1	3	2	9	5	4
Brunei Darussalam	4	2	3	4	13	6	7
Cambodia	3	1	3	2	9	5	4
People's Republic of China	7	2*	5	10	23	6	17
Indonesia	4	2	4	6	16	6	10
Japan	6	3	6	4	17	11	6
Republic of Korea	5	1	5	11	22	8	14
Lao People's Dem. Rep.	5	1	3	2	11	6	5
Malaysia	5	2	8	4	19	7	12
Myanmar	3	1	4	2	10	5	5
Philippines	3	2	3	4	12	6	6
Singapore	13	3*	12	5	32	8	24
Thailand	8	1	9	6	24	9	15
Vietnam	3	1	5	2	11	6	5
Total	30	7	39	33	109	23	86

(Continued)

Table 1: (Continued)

Negotiating body	Under Implementation	Signed	Under negotiation	Proposed	Total	Inside EA	Outside EA
Under Implementation						12	18
Signed						3	4
Under negotiation						3	36
Proposed						5	28

ASEAN = Association of Southeast Asian Nations, EA = East Asia (ASEAN+3).

The total avoids double counting and does not correspond to the vertical sum of agreements by status.

Notes on status of free trade agreements:

− Under negotiation = Under negotiation with or without a signed framework agreement.

− Proposed = Involved parties are considering creating an agreement, establishing joint study groups or joint task forces, and/or conducting feasibility studies for an agreement.

* negotiation concluded and to be signed between China and Singapore in 2008.

Source: Data from Asia Regional Integration Center; 2008 FTA Database. http://www.aric.adb.org (accessed June 2008).

Table 2: FTAs involving countries in East Asia (ASEAN+6).

	Japan	ROK	China	ASEAN	India	Australia	N.Z.
Japan		⊙		✓	⊙	⊙	⊘
ROK	⊙		⊘	✓	⊙	⊘	⊘
China		⊘		✓	⊘	⊙	✓
ASEAN	✓	✓	✓	✓	✓*	✓*	✓*
India	⊙	⊙	⊘	⊙			
Australia	⊙	⊘	⊙	⊙			✓
N. Z.	⊘	⊘	✓	⊙		✓	

Note: ✓ concluded ⊙ under negotiation ⊘ under consideration N.Z. = New Zealand * to be signed in 2008.
Source: Updated from *Developing a Roadmap Toward East Asian Economic Integration*. ERIA JRP Series No. 1, 2007.

example, in the context of APEC, known as FTAAP was proposed, consisting of all APEC members.[9]

II. Main Features of FTAs in East Asia

1. *General characteristics*

The AFTA started with Common Effective Preferential Tariff (CEPT) agreement which only covered trade in goods; the agreement for trade in services and agreement for investment were concluded later. This gradual approach differs from the all-inclusive approach of the agreement, which was formulated from the outset as comprehensive agreements that included investment, services, property rights, customs harmonization, and other measures. This kind of practical approach reflects the developing nature of ASEAN and most of the other economies in East Asia.

The FTAs in East Asia vary extensively in terms of the institutional arrangements. AFTA followed a regional approach by adopting a CEPT with a different schedule for old members

---

[9] Asian Development Bank (2008). *Emerging Asian Regionalism: A Partnership for Shared Prosperity*. Manila, Asian Development Bank, p. 88.

and new members. It is also open for readjustment during the implementation.[10] The China–ASEAN framework agreement specifies a regional approach to negotiations, while providing for the possibility of bilateral negotiations, for example, in determining the lists of exemptions,[11] and a separated service and investment agreement were also negotiated. In contrast, Japan has followed both bilateral and regional approaches in negotiating its agreement with ASEAN.[12]

FTAs in East Asia used the term "comprehensive economic partnership" (CEP), which includes not just free trade, investment and service, but also many other areas, like IPR, standards, competition policy, procurement, labor mobility, and economic cooperation — this goes beyond traditional economic assistance, covering infrastructure, human resource development (HRD), capacity-building and technical assistance, etc. These agreements cover areas not yet covered or covered inadequately by the WTO, thus are commonly known as "WTO Plus".

Liberalization is the major part of FTA. It covers elimination of tariffs and non-tariff barriers; national treatment of imports; market access for trade in services; investment liberalization through national treatment; and national treatment in government procurement. There are schedules for liberalization, exclusion and negative lists, and accelerated liberalization through early harvest programs. However, some protection measures are made in the FTA agreement that include safeguard measures on disruptive imports, fair competition between imports and domestically-produced goods,

---

[10] AFTA has experienced several changes. In 1996, the time frame was changed from 15 years to 10 years and tariff reduction target from 0–5% to zero; in 1999, the time frame was changed again, for old members 2010, for new members, 2015 (except few sensitive goods).

[11] Tubagus Feridhanusetyawan (2005). Preferential Trade Agreements in the Asia-Pacific Region. *IMF Working Paper* 05149, pp. 15–16.

[12] An interesting case in the Japan-Philippines FTA finds that there is provision for entry and temporary stay of nurses and certified care-workers from the Philippines to Japan.

protection of intellectual property rights, investment guarantees, and dispute settlement mechanisms.

Considering the differences of FTA members, the agreement provides flexible and special treatment for the less developed CLMV countries. They can take the form of delayed timeframes in fulfilling commitments, larger sensitive and exclusion lists, and special assistance in capacity-building such as human resource development and infrastructure development.[13]

Facilitation arrangements are usually included in the FTA package. They include customs valuation and procedures, standards and conformance measures dealing with the technical barriers to trade, and sanitary and phyto-sanitary measures; rules of origin as criteria to preferential treatment; transparency of laws and regulations; movement of professional and business people; and improvements in logistics and transportation.

Economic cooperation becomes an integrated part of FTA that includes a wide range of issues like macroeconomic dialogue and surveillance mechanisms; financial and monetary cooperation, infrastructure development, sub-regional development, human resource development and capacity-building, cooperation in development of small and medium enterprises, cooperation in science and technology development and research and development etc.

FTAs in East Asia seek for a freer trade and investment situation instead of a real economic "integration-oriented" approach. This shows that what East Asia needs and can do at this stage is to improve the regional business environment and promote inner cohesiveness of the market. Even the proposed EAFTA or CEPEA have goals focusing on market openings rather than economic cohesion. ASEAN has decided to establish an economic community (AEC) by 2015, which aims at creating a single market and production base. It seems that the main goal of AEC, at least at

---

[13] See *Toward an East Asian FTA: Modality and Roadmap*. A report by Joint Expert Group on feasibility study of EAFTA, September 2006.

planning this stage, is still a high-level liberalized market space rather than high-level economic integration based on integrated economic policies and institutions.[14]

2. *Tariff reduction*

Tariff reduction is no doubt an important and essential chapter in most agreements of FTAs in East Asia, but there seems to be no common practice and extensively accepted example to undertake tariff reduction. Some agreements, such as AFTA, ACFTA, AKFTA, Singapore–New Zealand FTA, and Singapore–Australia FTA, have pursued a negative list approach, by which tariffs for all items are generally reduced and sensitive goods are listed on the sensitive track and subject to some specific arrangements. In contrast, AJFTA, JSEPA, and some other FTAs take a positive list approach, whereby tariffs of all items including specific commodities on the list are reduced according to a detailed tariff reduction schedule.

In all these agreements, there is a common practice that members set the base tariff rates to which the reduction applies before tariff reduction schedules are adopted. The base rate is usually the MFN-applied rate at the beginning of the negotiation period (see Table 3).

With the negative list approach, specific goods would usually be listed under "sensitive track" or "highly sensitive track" with a specific tariff reduction schedule consisting of a transitional period or specific tariff rate. There is an exception list including some items, even sectors, which are exempt from tariff commitment. Although the positive list approach differs by way of appearance, there is also exemption in the agreement.

Most FTA agreements usually have some transitional periods for less developed countries. Even when the signatories are developed economies, there are specific arrangements for specific items

---

[14] AEC intends to be a single market and production base, a highly competitive economic region, a region of equitable economic development and a region fully integrated into the global economy.

Table 3: Tariff reduction in selected East Asian FTAs.

AFTA	ACFTA	AJFTA	AKFTA	JSEPA	CNZFTA
Negative list approach, zero % target. The CEPT scheme allows countries to maintain a temporary exclusion list (TEL), sensitive list (SL), and general exclusion list (EL). Commodities are phased into inclusion list (IL) gradually, and there is a longer timeframe for ASEAN4 countries. ASEAN6 reached	Negative list approach. Under the normal track, tariff will be eliminated by 2010 for ASEAN6 and China. Under the sensitive track, tariff reduction will start in 2012, to reach 0–5% tariff levels by 2018. ASEAN4 is given five more years after ASEAN6 to follow a similar tariff reduction scheme. Tariff on goods under the Early	Positive list approach. Japan formulated different agreements with ASEAN members. Most tariffs will be eliminated immediately or reduced to 0–5% in 11 years for ASEAN6. ASEAN4 is subject to 18 years to follow a similar scheme. (But Vietnam has to conduct a relatively serious	Negative list approach. Under the normal track, tariff will be eliminated by 2010 for ASEAN6 and China. ASEAN4 is given 8 more years after ASEAN6 to follow a similar tariff reduction scheme. (Vietnam is given 6 more years) Under the sensitive track, tariff reduction will	Positive list approach. Tariff on Singapore's imports from Japan will be zero immediately. To complete tariff elimination in Japan with 10-year transition period by 2010. Japan maintains some exceptions, including meat and meat products,	Positive list approach. Tariff on N.Z imports from China will be zero % no later than 2016. China has 3 more years to commit the scheme by 2019. China maintains some exceptions, including greasy wool, carbonized wool, carded wool and 6 other

(Continued)

Table 3: (*Continued*)

AFTA	ACFTA	AJFTA	AKFTA	JSEPA	CNZFTA
0-5% tariff in 2003, Vietnam in 2006, Lao PDR and Myanmar in 2008, and Cambodia in 2010.	Harvest Program, which includes agricultural products (Chapters 1 to 8 of the HS code), will be reduced to zero for ASEAN6 and China.	schedule). Japan has a 16-year scheme to eliminate tariff to zero or reduce to a low line of less than 20%. There are also some specific items in the list which are excluded from any tariff commitment.	start in 2012, to reach 0-5% tariff levels by 2016 for ASEAN6 and Korea, by 2021 for Vietnam, and by 2024 for ASEAN3.	fruit and vegetables, dairy products, and cane and beet sugar.	items. The tariffs on the products in Chapters 44, 48 and 49, shall have rates applied in accordance with China's WTO commitments. There is an Accelerated Tariff Elimination clause of Article 8 in the agreement.

Note: CNZFTA = China-New Zealand Free Trade Agreement.
Source: Summarized from FTA agreements.

or sectors; like in the JSEPA, Japan enjoyed a transitional period and gradual tariff reduction before giving market access to Singapore. ACFTA started with an Early Harvest Program (EHP), tariffs for 600 agricultural products were eliminated ahead of an FTA, and China did not request a reciprocal reduction from ASEAN new members.

3. *Rules of origin*

ROOs vary from a local or regional content (VC, satisfying minimum local or regional value content) approach, to a change in tariff classification (CTC, defined at a detailed HS level) rule and a specific process (SP, requiring a specific production process for an item) rule. Most agreements allow for cumulative ROOs to determine the total bilateral or regional local content of a product. For example, the criterion of 40 percent VC was first introduced by AFTA when the CEPT scheme was agreed upon in 1992. During the negotiation for an FTA between China and ASEAN, China accepted the AFTA ROOs.

JSEPA specifies a "wholly obtained or produced entirely" rule. It says that products should undergo sufficient transformation in the member country to receive preferential treatment in the FTA. Cumulation and *De Minimis* are accepted but the agreement specifies different shares of *De Minimis* with it being set at 8–10 percent. Heading changes are required for HS01-24, HS38 (chemical products), HS85 (machinery), with sub-heading changes or regional contents requirements (liquor and cordials). A regional contents requirement of 60 percent (with a combination of sub-heading changes) is required for other chapters of HS. For textile fabrics and articles (HS59), fabric should be made with yarn from an FTA-member country.[15]

---

[15] Inkyo Cheong and Jungran Cho (2006). Market Access in FTAs: Assessment Based on Rules of Origin and Agricultural Trade Liberalization. *RIETI Discussion Paper Series* 07-E-016, pp. 10–11.

Table 4: Overview of ROO of FTAs in East Asia.

	AFTA	ACCEC	AJCEP	AKCEC	JSEPA	NCFTA
CTC	Yes, but not necessary	Yes, but not necessary	Yes	Yes	Yes	Yes
RVC Ratio	40%	40%	40%	60-40%	60-40%	50-30%
SP	Chp. 50-63	Chp. 50-63	Chp. 50-63	Not mentioned	Chp. 28-40, 50-63	Chp. 28-40, 50-63
Cumulation	Yes	Yes	Yes	Yes	Yes	Yes
De Minimis	Not mentioned	Not mentioned	7-10%	10%	8-10%	Not mentioned

Notes:
(1) CTC: change in tariff classification rule.
(2) RVC: regional value content rule.
(3) SP: specific process rule.
Source: Summarized from individual FTA agreements.

Table 5: ROOs of bilateral FTAs in East Asia (AEAN+6).

Value Added Criterion (VC)	
Singapore–New Zealand	Cumulative local content >40%
Singapore–Australia	Cumulative local content >50%
Australia–New Zealand	Cumulative local content >50%
Change of tariff code classification (CTC)	
Japan–Malaysia	HS 4-digit
Thailand–Australia	HS 4-digit or HS 6-digit
Thailand–New Zealand	HS 4-digit or HS 6-digit
Singapore–ROK	HS 4-digit or HS 6-digit
Alternative	
Japan–Singapore	Cumulative local content >40%, or CTC HS 4-digit
Requirement of VC and CTC	
Thailand–India	Cumulative local content >40%, and CTC HS 4-digit
Singapore–India	Cumulative local content >40%, and CTC HS 4-digit

Source: Preliminary report on Developing a roadmap toward East Asian economic integration. ERIA, November, 2007, p. 34.

4. *Economic cooperation*

FTAs in East Asia also contain a variety of commitments relating to economic cooperation in a number of areas. Cooperation agreements are typically popular in statement or framework agreement, but many of them have no specific workplan, schedule or review mechanism. Economic cooperation represents a kind of commitment to a deepening of bilateral relationship as well as the effort in narrowing development gaps between FTA parties, which contributes to promoting regional economic integration.

AFTA includes cooperation by way of the "Framework Agreements on Enhancing ASEAN Economic Cooperation" in 1992. ASEAN members reached their consensus in four areas of cooperation — cooperation in trade, cooperation in industry, minerals and energy, cooperation in finance and banking, cooperation in transportation and communications. They also agreed to increase cooperation in research and development, technology transfer,

tourism promotion, human resource development and other eco-
nomic-related areas.[16]

The China–ASEAN framework agreement enjoyed wide-range
cooperation commitments in which five key sectors were identified:
agriculture, information and communication technology, human
resource development, investment, and Mekong River basin development. Concrete measures were also listed in the areas of
promotion and facilitation of trade in goods, services, and investment (standards and conformity assessment, technical barriers to
trade/non-tariff measures and customs cooperation), enhancing
the competitiveness of SMEs, promotion of electronic commerce,
capacity-building and technology transfers.

The AJFTA also detailed many areas of cooperation including
trade facilitation, business environment, energy, information and
communications technology, human resource development,
tourism and hospitality, transportation and logistics, and standards conformity and mutual recognition. The AKFTA conducted
a long list of 19 cooperation areas ranging from customs procedures, trade and investment promotion, standards and conformity
assessment and sanitary and phytosanitary measures, and small
and medium enterprises to sectors of financial services, broadcasting and film.

Singapore attaches no significance to cooperation in her FTA
agreements. There is no cooperation in the agreement of JSEPA
in contrast with the contents of cooperation in CNZFTA. It is a
wide scenario of cooperation ranging from economic cooperation,
cooperation on small and medium enterprises (SMEs) to labor
and environmental cooperation. In pursuit of the objectives of
cooperation, two countries encourage and facilitate the following
activities: policy dialogue and regular exchanges of information
expand trade and investment; providing assistance and facilities

---

[16] O G Dayaratna Banda and John Whalley (2005). Beyond goods and services:
competition policy, investment, mutual recognition, movement of persons, and
broader cooperation provisions of recent FTAs involving ASEAN countries.
NBER Working Paper 11232, pp. 25–26.

to business persons and trade missions that visit each other's country; supporting dialogue and exchanges of experience; stimulating and facilitating economic activities of public and/or private sectors. Additional importance especially is attached to cooperation on SMEs. To achieve this objective, they will promote cooperation and information exchange between government institutions, business groups and industrial associations, hold trade fairs and investment marts, promote training and personnel exchange and help provide financial support and intermediary services to SMEs.[17]

5. *Commitments beyond tariff reduction*

There are some specific chapters about "Technical barriers to trade" including quantitative trade restrictions and other NTBs elimination in most East Asian FTA agreements, although the extent and the depth vary. Singapore tends to have fewer technical barriers than other nations in East Asia. For instance, Singapore–New Zealand FTA, JSEPA, and Singapore–Australia FTA state that quantitative restrictions are either not permitted or subject to WTO criteria. In contrast, AFTA, an FTA including economies ranging from the most developed to the least, still kept technical barriers as a "safeguard" to the less developed economies. As a matter of fact, most economies care about technical barriers.[18]

Like commitments to technical barriers, Singapore tends to have liberal content of safeguards in its FTA agreements, with no safeguards in the Singapore–New Zealand and Singapore–Australia FTAs. However, JSEPA, ACFTA, AKFTA, AJFTA and CNZFTA all mention that members have the right to initiate such a measure on a good within the transition period, though it varies. But AFTA did not mention safeguard content at all. In addition, there are also "Anti-dumping/countervailing duty management" chapters in

---

[17] See China–New Zealand Free Trade Agreement 2008.
[18] See Tubagus Feridhanusetyawan (2005).

most agreements of East Asian FTAs. But most of these FTAs do not go beyond the commitments of WTO.

All FTAs in East Asia cover the liberalization of services trade, although the extent of commitment and implementation vary. Many agreements include services liberalization in the agenda, but contain few provisions beyond General Agreement on Trade in Services (GATS) commitments. ASEAN Framework Agreement on Services (AFAS) follows the GATS positive list approach and promises to go beyond GATS in terms of liberalization. But the progress of AFAS has been very slow. JSEPA and Singapore–New Zealand agreements also follow such an approach besides a wider provision including market access, national treatment or MFN treatment. Sometimes, FTA agreement in services adopts the negative list approach as well, although few liberalization contents differ in nature like the Singapore–Australia FTA. The ASEAN+1 framework agreements, such as ACFTA, AJFTA and AKFTA, clearly note that each party is committed to liberalize trade in services beyond its GATS commitments. ACFTA and AKFTA formulated a detailed agreement in services while AJFTA postponed its liberalization of services trade and shall continue to discuss and negotiate provisions for trade in services. Like commitments of tariff reduction, agreements in services have a general list and an exemption list incorporating specific sectors.

The scope of each agreement needs to be examined in order to understand the main characteristics of each FTA deal. Hence, it is essential to first define the scope of the standard regulation. The standard scope of the regulation can easily be defined, since most of the nations involved in FTAs are also members of the WTO. According to this, the framework of FTA agreements can be categorized as market access for goods, service/investment, intellectual property, government procurement, and others, and institutional provision.[19]

---

[19] KIEP (2008). Papers presented for the International symposium on possible roadmap to a CJK FTA: Obstacles and Expectations, 1 August 2008, p. 6.

Table 6: Services and investment liberalization in selected East Asian FTAs.

	AFTA	ACCEC	AJCEP	AKCEC	JSEPA	NCFTA
Services	Services liberalization is covered under AFAS, signed in 1995. The objective of AFAS is to enhance cooperation in services, to eliminate substantially restrictions to trade in services, and to liberalize trade in services by expanding the depth and scope of liberalization beyond GATS	Agree to enter negotiation to progressively eliminate all discriminatory measures with respect to trade in services, expand the depth and scope of services liberalization under GATS, and enhance cooperation in services to improve efficiency and competiti-veness.	Liberalization is directed to progressive elimination of substantially all discrimination, expansion in depth and scope of services liberalization. Facilitation of entry and temporary movement of business people. Enhanced cooperation in services.	Agree to enter negotiation to progressively liberalize trade in services among the parties with substantial sectoral coverage in conformity with Article V of GATS. Such liberalization shall be directed to elimination of discriminatory	Positive list approach based on GATS. Mainly agreement on national treatment and improvement of market access. Safeguard provision is not included. Government procurement and investments are covered separately. The right	Mainly agreement on national treatment, MFN treatment and improvement of market access. Air traffic rights, and services directly related to the exercise of air traffic rights are generally excluded. Government procurement is not included.

(Continued)

Table 6: (Continued)

	AFTA	ACCEC	AJCEP	AKCEC	JSEPA	NCFTA
	commitment. AFAS follows a positive list approach.			measures, expansion in the depth and scope of liberalization of trade in services, enhanced cooperation in services among the parties in order to improve efficiency and competitiveness.	of non-establishment is not included. Maritime and aviation services are generally excluded, while telecommunications services are covered under separate chapter.	
Investment	Covered under the Framework Agreement on the ASEAN	The parties agree to enter into negotiation to	ASEAN and Japan decide to create to liberal and	The parties agree to enter into negotiation to	Provision of national treatment to investors and	National treatment and MFN treatment are

(Continued)

Table 6: (*Continued*)

AFTA	ACCEC	AJCEP	AKCEC	JSEPA	NCFTA
Investment Area (AIA), signed in 1998, to establish ASEAN competitive investment area by 2010 and free flow of investment by 2020. AIA provides national treatment to ASEAN investors by 2010 and other investors by 2020, opens all industries to ASEAN	progressively liberalize investment regime, to strengthen cooperation in investment, to facilitate investment, to improve transparency of investment rules and regulations, and to provide protection for investment.	competitive environment, to strengthen cooperation in investment, to facilitate investment, to improve transparency, and to provide protection for investor and investment.	progressively liberalize investment regime, to strengthen cooperation in investment, to facilitate investment, to improve transparency of investment rules and regulations, and to provide protection for investment.	equal access to justice to pursue or defend investor's right. No performance-related requirement as the condition for establishment and expansion of operation. Temporary safeguard measures are possible in the case of serious	included. Free transfer of all payments relating to an investment. Neither party shall expropriate or nationalize investment or other equivalent measures, Investors are protected against expropriation, and fair market value of the expropriated

(*Continued*)

Table 6: (Continued)

AFTA	ACCEC	AJCEP	AKCEC	JSEPA	NCFTA
investors by 2010 and others by 2020.				balance of payment difficulties. Neither party shall expropriate or nationalize investment or other similar measures, except for public purposes, and the expropriation shall be conducted based on non-discriminatory bases and upon the payment of compensation.	investment is compensated immediately should expropriation occur. Government procurement is excluded. Providing investor dispute settlement mechanism.

Source: Individual FTA agreements.

III. Needs a Wider Regional FTA

1. *New challenges*

"Spaghetti bowl" effects

East Asian economies are highly interdependent through a regional production network. This production network operates by separating a production chain into small parts and then assigning each to the most cost-efficient location. This means that production processes are fragmented into multiple slices and located in different countries in East Asia. Some steps take place within a single firm (or firms of the same group) that has operations in different countries, while others involve arm's length transactions among different firms in several countries.

East Asian FTAs started with a multi-layered approach. This approach can provide incentives for individual countries and sub-regional groups like ASEAN in realizing their best-expected gain. However, it may also create new barriers in regional trade and investment: the regional market becomes divided because of different arrangements, which will reduce the gains from the scale of the regional market; business cost will increase due to the complicated or contradicted regulations (for example, ROOs), which is counter-productive to the network-based economic integration.[20]

Complex FTAs could potentially disrupt the processes of cross-border production networks which have been central to the region's successful integration. Uncoordinated proliferation may lead to inconsistent provisions between FTAs, especially on the rules of origin, which could hamper the process of production networking across countries.[21]

The transaction costs may increase in terms of border-crossing procedures in an FTA. Costs can be attributed to documenting

---

[20] Zhang Yunling (2006). *Designing East Asian FTA: Rationale and Feasibility.* Beijing: Social Sciences Academic Press, pp. 7–8.

[21] Tubagus Feridhanusetyawan (2005). Preferential Trade Agreements in the Asia-Pacific Region. *IMF Working Paper* 05149, p. 31.

products and verifying them prior to border crossing. Continuous treatment of transactions across borders could be time-consuming and counter-productive, even to hinder the smooth mechanism in an FTA. As a result, many businessmen prefer paying MFN duties to proving origin which may cost them much more than money.

The "spaghetti bowl"[22] (or Asian noodle bowl) effect of FTAs exist for two reasons: one is that the scope and the models of tariff liberalization arrangements vary in each agreement, while the other is differences of ROOs. FTAs have different phase-in modalities, i.e. tariff reduction schedule, thus an exporter faces different tariff by destination. As for the ROOs, there are several types, and they are used differently even in the same agreement (see Tables 4 and 5).

Low utilization rates

Data shows that AFTA preferences were not being well used. Overall, less than three percent of intra-ASEAN trade benefited from AFTA's preferences (see Figure 1 below). In order to get

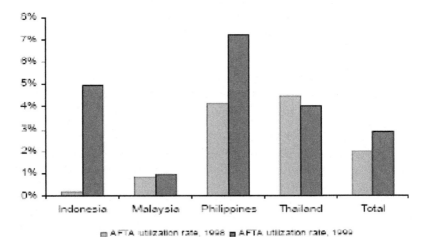

Source: PriceCooperWaterhouse. Presentation to the 10th Meeting of the ASEAN Directors-General of Customs, 24 July 2002.

Figure 1:   AFTA Utilization Rates (percent of Intra–ASEAN imports).

---

[22] See Bhagwati *et al.* (1998) and Panagariya (1999).

preferential tariff rate, the importers need to prove that the goods actually originated in ASEAN.[23] In AFTA, this requires "Form D." As it turns out, the vast majority of traders found it more advantageous either to pay the MFN-applied rate (and thus avoid the administrative cost and delay of Form D) or to take advantage of other schemes such as duty drawback programs or duty-free treatment in export processing zones.[24]

According to a JETRO survey, only 11.2 percent of Thailand's imports from AFTA took advantage of AFTA's CEPT. Malaysia's data indicates that only 4.1 percent of its exports to AFTA enjoyed the CEPT preference.[25]

What contributes to this low utilization rates under AFTA? The answer lies in the fact that AFTA's margins of preferential tariff versus MFN tariff rate on the majority of intra-trade are too small to compensate for the administrative cost and delay of applying for preferential tariff treatment. Due to the production networks, computer/machinery (HS chapter 84), electrical goods, and electronic parts and components (HS chapter 85) form the majority of intra-AFTA trade. The MFN tariff rates of the above items to US exporters are respectively 1.9 percent and 1.5 percent, 2.5 percent and 2.2 percent to EU, and the preferential tariff rates in AFTA are 1.5 percent and 1.4 percent. So the margins coming from AFTA are quite small, only 0.4 percent and 0.1 percent to US, 1.0 percent and 0.8 percent to EU.[26] It is no surprise that an importer in ASEAN will prefer a quick and convenient MFN tariff rate, given that the margins of preference are extremely low.

---

[23] To avoid tariff fraud, goods from third nations are transshipped through an ASEAN country to gain preferential access.

[24] Richard E. Baldwin (2007). Managing the Noodle Bowl: The Fragility of East Asian Regionalism. *ADB Working Paper series on regional economic integration* No. 7, pp. 12–13.

[25] JETRO (2003). *Current Status of AFTA and Corporate Responses*. Japan.

[26] Harrigan, F., W. James, M. Plummer and F. Zhai (2007). Bilateralism or Regionalism: Alternative Scenarios for Asian Trade Liberalization. Paper presented at the conference, Shaping the Future: Prospects for Asia's Long-term Development Over the Next Two Decades, December 2007, ADB Resident Mission, Bangkok.

Obviously, new challenges come along with the proliferation of FTAs in East Asia. A businessman may feel frustrated with having to face a variety of ROOs, regulations and other complex requirements which erode the naturally smooth mechanism of unilateral liberalization.

According to a more recent JETRO survey, which sampled more than 700 Japanese companies, 11.9 percent of them used FTAs, 22.8 percent of them plan to use, 37.4 percent of them do not plan to use. While SMEs have lower utilizing rate and planning utilizing rate, large companies tend to have higher utilizing and planning utilizing rate. The reasons for low utilization are:

— FTAs are not well known by firms.
— The phase-out tariff schedules make the impact of FTAs small.
— The administrative costs to prepare documents are costly: VC rule requires purchasing sources which frequently change.
— Exporters have to prepare documents, but benefits go to importers.
— It takes time to get certificate that does not match "just-in-time" production.
— FTAs will be utilized only for high volume and high MFN tariff products.

Additionally, IT-related products enjoy the benefit of Information Technology Agreement (ITA), and most intermediate goods for exports are exempted from the tariffs. This means that lots of traded goods in the East Asian production network have no tariff barriers.[27] According to a survey on Thailand firms, 45.7 percent of the sample (100 firms) used or plan to use tariff preferences. They are different for different sectors and sizes of the companies. In textile/garment sector, the utilization rate of FTAs for giant companies is 50 percent; for SMEs, 37.5 percent; in

---

[27] Dausuke Hiratsuka, Ikumo Isono and Hitoshi Sato (2007). Findings from Japan enterprises survey of the impact of FTAs: escaping from FTA trap and spaghetti bowl problem. JETRO-IDE, <www.ide.go.jp>.

Electronics, for giant companies, 85.7 percent; SMEs 32.2 percent; in Auto/auto parts sector, for giant companies, 57.1 percent; for SMEs, 31 percent. The non-utilization rate of FTAs is 26 percent; most of the companies responding are SMEs whose business have few connections on production network. Also, the utilization rates are different for different FTAs. For example, the companies showed more interest on Thailand–US FTA and Thailand–Japan EPA since these are related more to their business.[28]

2. Benefits of a wider regional FTA

In general, FTAs help to make rules and to develop the legal mechanism among countries in the region. The arrangements and agreements both at the bilateral or sub-regional levels are rule-making in nature in considering the principle of international standards, or being "WTO-consistent". In East Asian relations, this has profound significance since both "rule of standards" and "rule of law" will help to improve the systems of the regional members and to create a reliable foundation for the regional cooperation process. Thus, the regional arrangements will help to develop a new regional system based on increasing common or shared interests and rules among all parties. The institutional building in the region creates "public property" for countries in the region to maximize their interests.

Furthermore, from a dynamic perspective, the benefits from trade and investment facilitation, as well as economic cooperation under the framework of FTAs will extend beyond gains created by lowering tariffs. This new kind of regional economic cooperation in East Asia will improve the long-term environment for regional economic development.[29]

---

[28] Data from Ganeshan Wignaraja and Rosechin Olfindo (2008). FTA impacts on business activity in Thailand. ADB preliminary report presented at Asian "Noodle bowl" conference and technical workshop on impacts of FTAs on business activity in East Asia, 17–18 July Tokyo.

[29] Zhang Yunling (2006). *Designing East Asian FTA: Rationale and Feasibility*. Beijing: Social Sciences Academic Press, pp. 7–8.

However, as analyzed above, the complexity of FTAs makes business in the region also very costly. The competitive efforts in negotiating more FTAs by the regional countries may hurt the regional production network, which is essential for East Asian economic dynamism. Thus, a wider-regional FTA will help overcome most challenges including negative "Spaghetti bowl" (Noodle Bowl) effects. The estimations based on CGE modeling all show that for an FTA, the larger the size, the more the gains. The economic gains are significant if either moving toward EAFTA (ASEAN+3), or CEPEA (ASEAN+6) from current bilateral FTAs and ASEAN+1 FTAs.[30] Of course, a wider regional FTA is not a simple summary of current ASEAN+1 FTAs. It needs new negotiation though the current provisions in different FTAs could provide useful inputs to the wider regional FTAs.

IV. Thoughts on Deeper Regional Integration

1. *Toward an integrated regional FTA*

The problems of overlapping FTAs in East Asia has led to the recognition that an integrated regional FTA is needed. A preliminary political consensus was reached by ASEAN+3 Economic Ministers in 2004 that it was necessary to conduct a study on the feasibility of EAFTA. Under China's initiative, a joint expert group with members from 13 countries (ASEAN plus China, Japan and ROK) was set up in 2005. In a report to the ASEAN+3 Economic Ministers in September of 2006, the group insisted that the rationale for EAFTA lies in the interests of East Asian countries. The economic benefits from EAFTA exceed AFTA, any ASEAN+1 FTA, or other bilateral and sub-regional arrangements. The report recommended that EAFTA should be comprehensive, of a high standard and to be negotiated and implemented as a single undertaking. An

---

[30] According to the GTAP model, in case of EAFTA, there will be 1.93% of GDP increase; in the case of CEPEA, 2.05% GDP increase. See Report of the Track Two: Study on Comprehensive Economic Partnership in East Asia, 2008.

EAFTA should go beyond existing East Asian FTAs and be formed among ASEAN+3 countries first before opening up to other countries. The group urged East Asian leaders to start the process early.[31] The recommendations were not immediately accepted by ASEAN+3 leaders. The phase II study on EAFTA is still being led by ROK. However, for the future, ASEAN+3 remains a more feasible framework for starting a wider regional FTA in East Asia.

Japan proposed a different approach by calling a CEP based on the East Asia Summit (EAS) framework (CEPEA). EAS leaders agreed to conduct a feasibility study on CEPEA in 2006, and a joint expert group was established in 2007. A report completed in July 2008 and presented to an EAS ministers' meeting argued that a wider regional CEP including emerging India as a member will create larger gains than any other regional FTAs. The report recommended that CEPEA should provide a broader framework for regional integration and cooperation — with economic cooperation as the priority and an FTA as a core, covering facilitation, liberalization, environment and energy, as well as information and communication technology.[32] However, an EAS-based FTA may be even more difficult to achieve than other smaller frameworks.

In forging a wider regional FTA, ASEAN's willingness and consensus-building among its members are crucial. Establishing parallel ASEAN+1 FTAs ensures ASEAN's status which as a hub would best serve its interests. By moving towards an integrated regional FTA, ASEAN will loose its special status as a driver and a hub. Considering the big gaps among its members, ASEAN has to enhance itself as a real grouping with strong capacity to engage other economies more equally. ASEAN has set up the goal and agenda to establish a high-level community (economic, security and social) by 2015. It seems that ASEAN will probably only accept an integrated FTA in East Asia when it succeeds in building its

---

[31] Towards an East Asian FTA: modality and roadmap. A Report by Joint Expert Group for Feasibility Study on EAFTA, September 2006.

[32] Report of the Track Two: Study on Comprehensive Economic Partnership in East Asia, 2008.

economic community (AEC). So the best approach towards an East Asian FTA is to support and help ASEAN to realize the AEC first.

Three Northeast Asian countries — China, Japan and ROK — play a key role in constructing an East Asia-wide FTA because of their economic size and position in the region. The three economies are highly integrated through a FDI-trade network. Each of them has an FTA with ASEAN, but without any formal arrangement among themselves. If a Northeast Asian FTA could be realized ahead of EAFTA or CEPEA, then it could provide an easier and better foundation for East Asia to move towards a wider regional FTA. The leaders coming from the three countries agreed to launch a joint study in 2003, and the study group has finished its report on the feasibility of China-Japan-ROK FTA (CJK FTA). Although the conclusion to establish an FTA among the three countries is positive, the political momentum is difficult to build up because of Japan and ROK's worries on opening their agricultural markets to China. It is considered that CJK FTA looks like a long-term vision for the region and the plausible channel towards it could be through multiples of ASEAN+1 FTAs.[33]

The above analysis shows that an integrated FTA in East Asia is desirable, but it may not be realistic to expect it to be realized soon.

2. *Adopting best practices*

Considering the difficulties of moving towards an integrated FTA in East Asia, an alternative way is to standardize the FTAs by adopting "guiding principles" and following "best practices". In order to make them standardized, the FTA agreement should

---

[33] Hyungdo Ahn, (2006). FTA policies of CJK and prospect of CJK FTA: Korean Perspective. Paper presented on Prospects for Regional FTA in Northeast Asia, December 2006, Seoul. This view was also expressed by Motoshige Itoh who was involved in the joint study in his presentation at the same conference; see FTA policies of Northeast Asian countries and possibilities on Northeast Asian FTA: Japanese perspective. See the conference proceedings.

follow the multilateral disciplines, including comprehensive coverage in terms of measures, sectors and products, with few exemptions, liberal ROOs, effective monitoring and enforcement mechanisms to ensure consistent implementation. FTA's benefits derive from "best practices", which are reflected in comprehensive goods and service coverage, low and symmetrical rules of origin, best practices in customs procedures and related measures, strong trade-related intellectual property rights, national treatment of FDI, transparent and fair anti-dumping procedures and dispute settlement, open and non-discriminatory government procurement policies, competition policies creating a level playing field, as well as non-discriminatory and transparent technical barriers.

APEC has done the work on guiding principles for FTA best practice. The document detailed guiding lines for all major FTA covering provisions, including consistency of APEC's Bogor goals and WTO, comprehensiveness, commitments beyond WTO, transparency, facilitation, dispute settlement, rule of origin, cooperation, sustainable development, accession to the third market and periodic review.

By adopting best practices, the differences of FTA modalities may be largely reduced, which would make the modalities more transparent and disciplinary.

3. Harmonizing ROOs

Since multiple ROOs are becoming a problem for business in the region, it is necessary to find a way to solve this issue. ROOs should maximize trade creation and minimize trade distortion. One approach is to simplify ROOs so that they would be easier to understand and comply with. ROOs should be consistent across all of a country's FTAs.

However, simplification of ROOs by itself may be not a solution. It is considered that one way to enhance flexibility and reduce origin complexity would be to design co-equal rules of origin. This would give choices among a standardized tariff shift rule, RVC rule, or specific rule. It also could enhance existing cumulation provisions to full cumulation provisions by creating a regional standard and related regional implementation process for cumulation convergence.[34]

4. Facilitation

Considering the difficulties of moving towards a wider regional FTA, a facilitation agenda should be initiated to smooth the business transaction in the region. Aside from the proposed harmonizing of ROOs, an immediate step for reducing business cost is to adopt a single-window program in East Asia, either by extending ASEAN's single-window initiative to other East Asian countries, or agreeing on a single-window agreement among ASEAN+3 countries, or EAS members.

References

Ando, M. and F. Kimura (2005). "The Formation of International Production and Distribution Networks in East Asia". In *International trade*, T. Ito and A. Rose (eds.), Chicago: The University of Chicago Press.

Augier, P., M. Gasiorek and C. L. Tong (2005). The Impact of Rules of Origin on Trade Flows. *Economic Policy*, 43.

Bhagwati, J., D. Greenaway and A. Panagariya (1998). Trading Preferentially: Theory and Policy. *The Economic Journal* 108, pp. 1128–1148.

Feridhanusetyawan, T. (2005). Preferential Trade Agreements in the Asia-Pacific Region. *IMF Working Paper 05149*, pp. 13–31.

Harrigan, F., W. James, M. Plummer and F. Zhai (2007). Bilateralism or Regionalism: Alternative Scenarios for Asian Trade Liberalization. Paper presented at the conference. *Shaping the Future: Prospects for Asia's Long-term Development Over the Next Two Decades*, ADB Resident Mission, Bangkok.

---

[34] This recommendation came from the presentation paper, "Rules of origin & origin administration in East Asia", at the Asian noodle bowl conference, ADBI, 18 July 2008.

JETRO (2003). *Current Status of AFTA and Corporate Responses*, Japan.

Kawai, M. and G. Wignaraja (2008). Regionalism as an engine of multilateralism: A case for a single east asian FTA. Working Paper series on regional economic integration 14. ADB.

Lee, H. (2007). Regional Integration, Sectoral Adjustments and Natural Groupings in East Asia. OSIPP Discussion Paper: 2007-E-008, pp. 9–13.

Panagariya, A. and R. Dutta-Gupta (2001). "The 'Gains' from Preferential Trade Liberalization in the CGE Models: Where Do They Come From?". In *Regionalism and Globalization: Theory and Practice.* S. Lahiri (ed.), Routledge.

Plummer, M. G. (2007). Best Practices in Regional Trading Arrangements: An Application to Asia. *The World Economy* 30(12), pp. 1771–1796.

World Bank (2005). *Global Economic Prospects 2005: Trade, Regionalism, and Development.* Washington: World Bank.

CHAPTER 7

China's FTA Strategy: An Overview[1]

After its WTO accession, China began to be active in initiating regional trade arrangements (RTA). China considers that the regional markets are specially significant for its exports, and the regional members are important for developing good relations and cooperative partnership. It is clear that the RTA strategy has been used for both economic and strategic interests. As a WTO member, China follows WTO rule in negotiating and implementing FTAs.

I. Current Status

The priority of China's RTA strategy is the region where it is situated, i.e. the neighboring countries in ASEAN with which it signed its first FTA. Nevertheless, China has a global interest in selecting its FTA partners.

China has concluded 4 FTAs since[2]: China–ASEAN (goods, service), China–Pakistan FTA, China–Chile FTA (goods, service) and China–New Zealand FTA. China has conducted negotiations

---

[1] This paper was written for a conference on FTA Strategy in Asia organized by ADB Institute in Tokyo in 2008.

[2] Not including two CEPAs with Hong Kong and Macao that were considered as a special and internal market arrangement within China framework. The negotiation for China–Singapore FTA was concluded by September of 2008 and will be signed soon.

with GCC, Australia, Iceland, Norway, and Peru;[3] Track I studies with Costa Rica, and Track II studies on China–South African Custom Union, China–India and China–Republic of Korea (ROK). For regional agreements, China has participated in Asia–Pacific Agreement (tariff reduction only, including 6 countries–India, ROK, Bangladesh, Sri Lanka, Laos and China), GMS facilitation agreement and Track II studies on China–Japan–ROK (CJK) FTA, ASEAN+3 FTA (EAFTA) and CEPEA (East Asia Summit framework) (see Table 1).

For bilateral FTAs, the partners including developed and developing economics are globally selected based on mutual interest. China insists that by negotiating a FTA, its market economy status should be officially recognized.

Generally, China has adopted a gradual approach in negotiating agreements with its partners — first goods, then service and investment. China–ASEAN FTA and China–Chile FTA have used this approach, but for China–Pakistan FTA, an early harvest program was followed by an agreement including goods and investment. The China–New Zealand FTA is a comprehensive and single-packaged agreement.

For liberalization and facilitation, FTAs between developing economies are focus more on tariff and non tariff measures. But for one between a developed and developing economy, for example, the FTA between China and New Zealand, other policy and institutional issues, are included, like IPR, transparency, standards, competition policy etc. The newly signed China–Peru FTA is the first comprehensive package with a developing country including trade in goods, service and investment.

Unfortunately, three major economies — US, EU and Japan — have not expressed their interest in an FTA with China yet since one major reason is China's request for a market economy status. Japan, for instance, is worried about agricultural liberalization with China.

---

[3] The negotiation was concluded on 19 November 2008. This is the first comprehensive package FTA.

Table 1: China's FTA initiatives with regional partners.

Initiative	Schedule	Partners
CEPA	2003, Signed in 2005	Hong Kong, China
CEPA	2004, Signed in 2005	Macao, China
China–ASEAN FTA	Framework agreement, 2002; Early harvest program, 2005; Trade in goods, 2005; service, 2007	ASEAN (10 members)
China–Pakistan FTA Early Harvest Program for the Free Trade	Signed in 2006 Signed in 2005	Pakistan
China–Chile FTA	Signed in 2005	Chile
China–New Zealand FTA	Negotiation from 2004, signed in 2008	New Zealand
China–Peru FTA	Negotiation from 2007, signed in 2008	Peru
China–GCC	Framework agreement in 2004, under negotiation	Gulf Cooperation Council (5 members)
China–Australia FTA	Negotiation from 2005	Australia
China–Iceland FTA	Negotiation from 2006	Iceland
China–Norway FTA	Negotiation from 2006	Norway
China–SACU FTA	Study from 2005	South African Customs Union (5)
China–ROK FTA	Study from 2006	Republic of Korea
China–Indian FTA	Study from 2005	India

II. Future Trend

China will continue its efforts on concluding more FTAs. The most feasible FTAs to be concluded in the near future may be: China–GCC, China–Norway, China–Costa Rica and also China–Australia.

East Asia is the region that has great significance for China which has made great effort in promoting its regional cooperation and integration. Economically, China is a key factor in the regional production network and has benefited remarkably from integration and cooperation. Thus, China will continue to initiate and

Table 2: Other regional economic initiatives.

Initiatives	Date of assignment	Partners
Asia–Pacific Trade Agreement (Bangkok Agreement)	2005	Republic of Korea, India, Bangladesh, Lao People's Democratic Republic (Lao PDR)
East Asia FTA	Initiated Study, Report completed in 2006	ASEAN, Japan, ROK
SCO FTA	Proposed in 2005	Shanghai Cooperation organization members (5 members)
FTAAP	Initiated by US in 2006	APEC members
Greater Mekong Sub-region, Strategic Frame of Facilitation on Trade and Investment	2005	Cambodia, Lao PDR, Myanmar, Thailand and Vietnam
Joint Declaration on the Promotion of Tripartite Cooperation	2003	Japan and Republic of Korea
ACD (Asia Cooperation Dialogue)	2002	21 members

Sources: Ministry of Commerce of the People's Republic of China, www.mofcom.gov.cn and Ministry of Foreign Affairs of China, www.fmprc.gov.cn

participate in the regional arrangements. Aside from China–ASEAN FTA, China also has strong interest to promote EAFTA (10+3) (see Tables 2 and 3). The major reasons for are: (1) The major economic integration (production network) has been made among those economies; (2) The progress of the three "10+1" FTAs are faster than the other "10+1" FTAs (ASEAN–CER, ASEAN–India) since all three "10+1" FTAs have already been concluded (except investment agreements for ASEAN–China and ASEAN–ROK); (3) ASEAN+3 has a stronger political structure than the East Asia Summit with its more than 10 years experience since 1997; (4) An early start of EAFTA could encourage India to

Table 3: Feature of FTAs signed between China and its partners.

	EHP	Trade in goods	Trade in service	Investment	Approach
China–ASEAN	Agricultural goods	2005	2007	Not yet	Two tracks, Gradual
China–Chile	No	2005	2008	Not yet	3-year review
China–Pakistan	Comprehensive	2005, 2006	Not including	Including	5-year review
China–New Zealand	No	2008	2008	2008	One package
China–Peru		2008	2008	2008	One package

make more concessions in negotiation with East Asian partners who seem too conservative in liberalizing its market. However, an early start of EAFTA negotiation may have its difficulty given ASEAN's focus on its own community-building and Japan's different strategy on the East Asia FTA by proposing CEPEA (10+6).[4]

China also promotes a China–Japan–ROK FTA in Northeast Asia. The most integrated economies in East Asia are among China, Japan and ROK. The three countries have developed a high-level economic network through FDI-led economic exchanges for trade, service and other activities. China is the largest market for both Japan and ROK in their external trade and the largest FDI market for ROK and second largest for Japan. China believes that a CJK FTA will give its market access to Japan and ROK. The Track II study (the academic study) for CJK FTA has been conducted for three years and the conclusion shows that the three countries will benefit significantly from it. Unfortunately, political consensus has not been reached for an early start though the three countries have agreed that an investment agreement should be negotiated first which may set the foundation for negotiations of trade in goods and service, as well as economic facilitation and cooperation.[5] China also participated in the Track II study but is cautious on an early start of CEPEA based on "1+6." The study concluded that it has lots of constraints since the priority should be given to economic cooperation and facilitation, though the CGE simulation shows a larger gain from CEPEA than EAFTA.

A FTAAP initiative was made by the US government during the leaders' meeting of APEC in 2006. China considered it to premature negotiate a FTA in such a large region of the Asia-Pacific though it has actively participated in APEC activities.

---

[4] Zhang Xiaojing (2008). Network of FTAs surrounding China. *Journal of Asia-Pacific Review*, 4, p. 20.

[5] Japan seems not to be in hurry to initiate CJK FTA and has put it as a long-term item on the agenda. See Zhang Baoren and Xu Yongmei (2008). China-Japan economic relations and its future. *Northeast Study*, 2, p. 31.

Due to many factors, the speed of negotiations for more FTAs between China and other partners would slow down not because of China losing its interest, but because of its partners having different priority of FTA strategies, or facing constraints from social pressure (liberalization of the agriculture sector) and threat from the competition.

III. CAFTA as a Case

China started its regional strategy with China–ASEAN FTA (CAFTA). The question was raised on the motivation behind it. Why did China initiate the China–ASEAN FTA (CAFTA) first?

China chose CAFTA for a start mainly because of an "easier first" practical approach. China and ASEAN have shared increasing interests in their trade and economic relations. For China, a FTA with ASEAN will enable Chinese companies to enter the ASEAN market easily, which can also be an experiment in participating in and promoting regional integration and cooperation after joining the WTO. China is more confident of making a FTA with ASEAN partners than with Japan or ROK.[6]

Considering the internal differences of ASEAN, liberalization has been achieved by different tracks and on different timetables.

For service liberalization, the commitments of both parties are greater than their WTO ones (for new members of ASEAN, no more than WTO requirements). The new liberalization agenda is to be negotiated one year after the implementation of the agreement. However, there are several sectors that are excluded from the liberalization agenda and lots of areas are unbounded even in the liberalized sectors (see Tables 4 and 5).

FTA is just a core part of the framework agreement. It also lists other areas for broad cooperation with five areas listed as priority sectors: agriculture; information and communications technology;

---

[6] Political gains are also important for China since a closer economic relationship helps to smooth the comprehensive relations between the two sides, which has significant dimension in creating a peaceful environment surrounding China.

Table 4:   China–ASEAN FTA for trade in goods (enforced in 2005-7).

I. Principles
    (1) Early harvest program
    (2) Tariff reduction: gradual, but with time table, two tracks for ASEAN — old
        members, new members
    (3) ROO, accumulation VC 40%
    (4) Trade dispute settlement

II. Liberalization
    (1) EHP 600 agri. products zero tariff (2006, 2009)
    (2) 93% of products zero tariff by 2010 new members, 2015, 2012
        (new members, 2018)
    (3) Sensitive products, not more than 10%, tariff <20% by 2012 (2018), <5% by
        2015 (2020), for highly sensitive products <50% by 2015 (2018)

human resources development; investment; and GMS. Cooperation
has covered many areas including banking, finance, tourism, industrial cooperation, transport, telecommunications, intellectual
property rights, small and medium enterprises (SMEs), environment, bio-technology, fishery, forestry and forestry products,
mining, energy and sub-regional development. In order to adjust
their economic structure and expand their trade and investment
with China, capacity-building programs and technical assistance
have be implemented, particularly for the newer ASEAN member
states. A profound significance of the economic integration between
China and ASEAN is to establish legal systems for trade, investment
and management following WTO rules and international standards.

IV. Impacts of FTA

FTAs should be considered as the supplement to WTO since they
are featured as "WTO plus" which means that their liberalization
commitments are realized faster than those on the WTO agenda,
and their programs have more coverage.

The FTA promotes trade, service and investment since it provides an improved environment for business between the partners.
For example, the EHP program between China and ASEAN has

Table 5: China–ASEAN service (enforced in 2007–8).

I. Principles
  (1) China makes a single schedule of specific commitments, while each ASEAN member country makes its individual schedule of specific commitments
  (2) WTO-consistent
  (3) National treatment
  (4) Progressive liberalisation; review and initiating new negotiation; Flexibility, capacity-building for CLMV
  (5) Dispute settlement mechanism
  (6) Emergency safeguard measures

II. China's liberalization commitment areas (excluding some exceptions and limitations):
  (1) Computer and related services
  (2) Real estate services
  (3) Business services: market research services, management consulting services, services related to management
  (4) Construction and related engineering services
  (5) Environment service (excluding environmental quality monitoring and pollution source inspection)
  (6) Recreational, cultural and sporting service (excluding audio-visual services, golf)
  (7) Transport service: aircraft repair and maintenance services (joint venture), computer reservation system services (cooperating with China service)
  (8) Road transport services (including maintenance and repair services of motor vehicles)

III. Exclusion
  (1) Financial services
  (2) Government procurement
  (3) Air services

helped to increase agricultural trade between them. Such is the case with the China–Thailand EHP, where China's share in Thailand's agricultural export rose from 8.8 percent in 2003 to 13.4 percent in 2006. The China–ASEAN trade in goods has increased significantly in recent years, with an average growth rate of more than 30 percent. The FTA has made this possible, given the Chinese economic boom and their increasing production network from the growth of FDI both in ASEAN and China. From 2001–2007, trade in goods between China and ASEAN increased more than 20 percent annually. China's imports from ASEAN increased faster than its exports. Currently, ASEAN is the third largest import market for China. Strikingly, "high tech goods" (mostly electronics and automobile parts) accounted for 53 percent of imports from ASEAN. The FTA's boost to (FDI in China and ASEAN) must not be assumed since data on the growth of trade in goods between China and ASEAN may be misleading. For example, the growth rate of trade in goods was lower during 2005–2006 (after implementation of trade in goods) than during 2003–2004 (before implementation); FDI from China to ASEAN has increased significantly before the FTA. This means that the effect of FTA should not be over-estimated due to low usage of FTA in trade.[7]

Theoretically, FTA may create trade and investment diversion. In fact the negative effects may not be very obvious for trade and investment between ASEAN–China, ASEAN–Japan and ASEAN–ROK although three ASEAN+1 FTAs have been negotiated and signed (see Table 4). Trade and investment between China, Japan and ROK also seem unaffected by "10+1" FTAs. The slowing-down trend of trade between ASEAN and Japan, as well as between ASEAN and ROK, may not be a result of trade and investment diversion. The main factors affecting trade and investment between ASEAN+three countries (China, Japan and ROK) are the differential structures of their markets and economies, in general.

The FDIs from Japan and ROK in ASEAN and China should benefit from the China–ASEAN FTA since it helps the division of production in ASEAN and China.

Furthermore, a large share of the trade between ASEAN–China, ASEAN–Japan and ASEAN–ROK have not benefited from lowered tariffs since the tariff rates are already very low (weighted average rate below 5 percent or even no tariff for manufacturing parts). Noticeably, IT products already enjoy free tariff due to the WTO IT agreement.

---

[7] Li Hong (2008). Analysis and Perspective of China–ASEAN trade in goods, 2007–2008. *Around Southeast Asia*, 2, pp. 37–40.

Table 6: Growth rate of China's trade with major partners (%).

China	2002	2003	2004	2005	2006	2007
ASEAN						
Total	31.1	42.8	35.3	23.1	23.4	25.9
EX	22.3	31.1	38.7	29.1	28.8	32.0
IM	34.4	51.7	33.1	19.0	19.4	21.0
Japan						
Total	16.2	31.1	25.7	9.9	12.5	13.8
EX	7.8	22.7	23.7	14.3	9.1	11.4
IM	25.0	38.7	27.3	6.5	15.2	15.8
ROK						
Total	22.8	43.3	42.5	24.3	20.0	19.1
EX	23.8	29.4	38.4	26.2	26.8	26.1
IM	22.2	51.0	44.3	23.4	16.9	15.6
US						
Total	20.8	30.0	34.3	24.8	23.9	15.0
EX	28.9	32.2	35.1	30.4	25.5	14.4
IM	3.9	24.3	31.9	9.1	19.2	17.2
EU						
Total	15.4	44.1	33.9	22.6	26.0	27.0
EX	20.3	49.7	38.8	34.1	30.0	29.1
IM	10.4	37.7	27.8	5.0	19.1	22.4

Source: Calculated from statistics data, www.mofcom.gov.cn

East Asia intra-regional trade is high on vertical products because of the production network. But a large part of trade and investment in East Asia just follow the three "10+1" routes, i.e. ASEAN–China, ASEAN–Japan and ASEAN–ROK. Those that cross the "10+1" route are limited (except China–Japan–ROK). As a matter of fact, major factors affecting intra-regional flows of trade in goods, services and investments are government policy (business policy environment), operation cost (transportation) and market size (final sale). FTAs do not seem to be a major factor for business decisions yet.

Nevertheless, the effects of rule of origin (ROO) should be considered. In China–ASEAN FTA, a 40 percent accumulated ROO is adopted. This should help companies to benefit from the FTA, especially for those that have production networks between China and ASEAN. The real problem of ROO for companies in the region seem to be the complexity and added cost of documentation. Different FTAs have adopted systems (CTC, VC, SP) and different requirements. Even the same product, due to the different locations of the production process, is treated differently in different FTAs. In the China-ASEAN FTA, three systems of ROO are adopted (for most goods, VC are used). The requirement of accumulating VC is not difficult to reach, but the documentation is actually very complex. CTC may seem simple for most goods, but may not reach the requirement for change.

East Asia has been characterized by multi-layered FTAs that seem counter productive to the existing production network which is essential to the dynamics of the regional economies. A few more options may be necessary to deal with those problems.

Ideally a larger regional FTA promote, i.e. to establish a region-wide FTA in East Asia. Currently, there are two proposals: one is EAFTA, another is CEPEA. As mentioned above, the more feasible approach is to start from "ASEAN+3" through a negotiation based on three "10+1" FTAs, and then to extend it to other EAS members. However, it seems that the political consensus for such a big step will be very difficult to reach both because of ASEAN community-building and the current economic difficulties.

Considering the difficulty of reaching consensus among East Asian countries, it is desirable to initiate a facilitation agreement starting with a single window, mutual recognition of standards, harmonization of ROO and FDI promotion to less developed areas which may be considered as an EAFTA early harvest program.

References

Agreement on Trade in Goods of the Framework Agreement on Comprehensive Economic Co-operation ("The Framework Agreement") between China and ASEAN, November 2005.

Agreement on Trade in Services of the Framework Agreement on Comprehensive Economic Co-operation ("The Framework Agreement") between China and ASEAN, 14 January 2007.

ERIA (2008). Developing a roadmap toward East Asian economic integration.

Framework Agreement on Comprehensive Economic Co-operation ("The Framework Agreement") between China and ASEAN, 4 November 2002.

Free Trade Agreement between the government of the People's Republic of China and the government of the Republic of Chile, 18 November 2005.

The supplementary agreement on Trade in Services of the Free Trade Agreement between the government of the People's Republic of China and the government of the Republic of Chile, 13 April 2008.

CHAPTER EIGHT

Designing East Asian FTA: Rational and Feasibility[1]

East Asia cooperation and integration has made noticeable progress. The process, starting from 1997, has been marked by the following achievements: an institutional framework for regional cooperation set up through annual leaders', ministers' and senior officials' meetings; real progress in financial cooperation via the Chiang Mai Initiative; preferential trade arrangements (PTAs), like AFTA, China–ASEAN FTA, Japan–Singapore closer economic partnership agreement (CEP), as well as sub-regional development projects. The emergence of East Asian regionalism leading to regional institution-building brings the regional operation a step closer to the East Asian community.

I. Emerging Trend of FTA

The basic reason for regionalism is that it provides greater and better market access for the countries in the region through free trade arrangement (FTA). Compared with the multilateral approach, a regional arrangement is much more flexible and faster to implement since problems that would take years to solve in global negotiations can be dealt with much quicker. PTA, also known as CEP, can address areas not yet covered or covered

---

[1] This was written for the joint research project of IDE, JETRO and Institute of Asia-Pacific Studies, CASS on EAFTA in March 2005.

poorly by WTO arrangements, thus it is known as a WTO-Plus. Based on the current agreements made, the following areas are usually included:

1. Liberalization

— Market access for trade in goods through eliminating tariffs.
— National treatment of imports from partner countries.
— Reducing non-tariff measures on trade, e.g. import and export restrictions.
— Investment liberalization, providing national treatment.
— Market access for trade in services, opening service sector.
— Liberalizing service sector.

2. Facilitation

— Standards and conformance measures dealing with technical barriers to trade, and sanitary measures.
— The movement of natural and business persons.
— Rules of origin, imposing value-added percentages as criteria to preferential treatment.
— Transparency of laws and regulations.
— Safeguard measures, through restricting imports.
— Dispute settlement procedures, dispute-settling through consultations, conciliation, mediation or good offices before resorting to arbitration.
— Protecting intellectual property rights.
— Fair competition between imports and domestic produced goods.

3. Cooperation

— Economic and technical cooperation.
— Training and capacity building.
— Infrastructure, environment, development projects.

As matter of fact, the role of PTAs is not just to provide gains in market access, but also efficiency through competition. In many cases, PTA was used as a strategy for the policy-makers to facilitate reform and restructuring.

Furthermore, if regionalism goes in the direction of becoming an integrated regional institution, it may increase bargaining power in international (WTO) trade negotiations.

East Asian regionalism started to emerge essentially after 1997, i.e. after the Asian financial crisis. The crisis exposed the vulnerability of economic integration built only on market function and underlined the need for the strong regional cooperation to deal with the crisis and reduce future risks. However, the strengthening of economic integration in East Asia provides the foundation for progressive regionalism.

II. Economic Convergence in East Asia

Economic convergence in East Asia has transferred from a "flying geese model" to a regional network of production and services. The old model built up a "vertical" economic chain through capital flow, technology transfer and supply of manufacturing parts which created increasing intra-regional trade based on market exchange. During that period of time, there was little regional institution-building. ASEAN started its AFTA as early as in 1992, but its role as a leader in facilitating FTA in the East Asian region was marginal since its early goal of liberalization aimed mainly at making its own internal environment attractive to FDI.

The 1997 financial crisis was an important turning point since it changed both the environment and the structure of East Asian economic growth and integration. Due to the long stagnation of its economy and the negative impact of the financial crisis, Japan was no longer the "locomotive" of East Asian economic growth, thus, bringing an end to the "flying geese model". South East Asia was plunged into serious recession and economic difficulties by the financial crisis and political instability.

But with China's continuous economic dynamism and increasing inward FDI flow, both the regional growth pattern and the convergence structure shifted. A broader network of production and services gradually developed with increasing share of exchanges of parts, components and other intermediate products, reflecting the development of intricate intra-regional production networks in which production processes are subdivided among many different countries.[2] FDI flows play a key role in creating this network based on exchange of trade and capital which has profound impact on East Asian economic development since it has created a "parallel development" for the region. This is different from the traditional "flying geese model" based on the vertical and hierarchical transfer of technology. The FDI-driven supply chain has extended the structure of East Asian economic relations beyond market integration to the need for government cooperation and institution-building.[3]

Compared with other regions, East Asia is late in forging regional FTA and other institutional establishments. Aside from intra-regional desire for a closer partnership, East Asian region-alism is also considered to be a rational response to the progress of other regions, especially to the success of the EU and the establishment of NAFTA.[4] By definition, East Asian economic integration started as early as from the 1960s based on regional economic growth and only by market function, while the process of regional cooperation through regional institutional arrange-ment or government efforts began only from the late 1990s. The new initiative for regional cooperation will certainly help to enhance and facilitate further integration of the East Asian region.

---

[2] World Bank (2003). *East Asia Update: Looking beyond short-term shocks*, p. 15.

[3] Shujiro Urata argued for "a shift from market-led to institution-led regional economic integration in East Asia". Paper prepared for the Conference on Asian Economic Integration organized by Research Institute of Economy, Trade and Industry, Tokyo, Japan, April 22–23, 2002, p. 1.

[4] Prime Minister Mahathir's proposal of forming an East Asian Economic Caucus (EAEC) is considered a direct response to NAFTA. Peter Drysdale & Kenichi Ishigaki (ed.). (2002). *East Asian trade and financial integration, New issues*. Asia-Pacific Press, Canberra, p. 6.

III. FTAs in East Asia

Among all institutions, EAFTA is the most important. The road towards EAFTA starts from the multi-layered FTAs already in the region.

East Asia's, first FTA proposal was put forward in 1998 for a Japan–Korean FTA which is still under negotiation. More FTAs followed, both within East Asia, or with other countries; some have concluded, and some are still under negotiation.[5] The Japan–Singapore CEP (JSCEP) was a pioneer in making a new kind of FTA in the region since it covered more areas than traditional trade liberalization — i.e. trade, investment, services, the dispute settlement mechanism, and economic and technical cooperation on various functional levels between the two countries. But China took the lead in making a large-scale FTA between China and ASEAN as a group. The China–ASEAN CEP Agreement was signed in 2002, which started with an early harvest program focusing on liberalization of agricultural trade in goods and an agricultural cooperation agreement; the FTA agreement for trade in goods was signed in November of 2004. In 2003, Japan signed a CEP framework agreement with ASEAN and is now negotiating bilateral FTAs with some individual ASEAN economies (Thailand, Malaysia, Philippines) and preparing an overall agreement with ASEAN as a group. Aside from the negotiation with Japan, ROK decided to follow China and Japan to start negotiation with ASEAN in 2005.

The scope of FTAs or CEPs varies. Aside from liberalizing goods for trade, most are committed to facilitating trade, harmonizing quality and other regulatory issues, building infrastructure and streamlining customs procedures. Liberalization of trade in services and investment are also considered. Usually, there are also

---

[5] For East Asian non-East Asian agreements that have been concluded, see Singapore–US FTA, Korea–Chile FTA, Japan–Chile and Japan–Mexico FTA, Singapore-Australia FTA, Thailand–US FTA. China is currently negotiating FTA with Chile, Pakistan, New Zealand, as well as the Gulf Economic Cooperation Council. ASEAN is now negotiating FTA with CER and India.

provisions for human resource development (HRD) and technical assistance.

More importantly, the role for East Asian FTA or CEP is to make rules and develop the legal mechanism among countries in the region. The arrangements and agreements both on the bilateral or sub-regional levels are rules made on the principle of international standards, or made to be "WTO-consistent". In East Asian relations, this has profound significance since both "rule of standards" and "rule of law" will help to improve the systems of regional members and create a reliable foundation for the regional cooperation process. Thus, the regional arrangements will help to develop a new regional system based on increasingly common or shared interests and rules among all parties. The institution-building in the region creates "public property" for countries in the region to maximize their interests.

IV. Need for an Integrated Approach

Due to its diversity, East Asia started its FTA with a multi-layered approach. This approach provides incentives for individual countries and sub-regional groups like ASEAN to realize their best expected gain. However, it also creates new barriers in regional trade and investment in the following ways:

— The regional market becomes divided because of different arrangements, which will reduce any gain from the scale of the regional market.
— Business costs will increase due to the complicated or contradictory regulations (for example, rules of origins), which are counter-productive to the network-based economic integration.
— The region will not be able to realize its goal of community-building without an integrated regional market.

A theoretical study shows that a larger FTA can create more benefits than a smaller one. That is to say, the benefits of EAFTA would exceed any other FTA, whether bilateral FTA, or AFTA, or any "10+1" FTA. The study shows that every country will gain from EAFTA which is built on the high-level integration characterized by FDI-trade network relations. But the potential of the integration is far from being fully realized due to either by tariff barriers or non-tariff measures.

Calling for an integrated approach in moving towards EAFTA does not invalidate existing bilateral arrangements. It is to search for a feasible roadmap to arrive at the EAFTA.

V. Road Map to EAFTA

EAFTA can bring benefits to all members in the region. The foundation of EAFTA has been gradually built up through the following developments:

Firstly, economic integration is increasing. This encourages all members of the region to consider the feasibility of an EAFTA. Close economic integration has resulted in two effects: one is economic interdependence and also common interests, while the other is desire for market liberation so that economic transactions can be faster and more efficient. Currently, a new regional network of production and service has been developed, based on increasing intra-regional FDI flow, which has further enhanced the level of integration and common interests. Economic integration also calls for strengthening of government cooperation in providing a better environment for economic development and reducing market risk and preventing from the crisis. The business community is actively pressing their governments to more faster towards the regional FTA.

Secondly a multi-layered framework of sub-regional and bilateral FTAs may serve as a kind of capacity-building in rule-making and good governance for the region. This is an essential for a pan-regional FTA in the future since almost all countries in the region have no previous experience in forging any regional trade and investment arrangement (RTIA). Due to its great diversity, East Asian trade and investment arrangements have to be gradual and flexible. Currently, we have witnessed three different structures in RTIAs: the developed with the developed economies, represented by Japan–Singapore CEP, Japan–ROK (to be concluded); the developed with the developing economies, represented by Japan–ASEAN countries (with individual economies as well as with ASEAN as a whole in future) and the developing with the developing economies, represented by China–ASEAN FTA. These different types of arrangements provide rich experiences for negotiating an integrated regional FTA in the future.

The above factors help East Asian countries to build up consensus on moving towards an EAFTA. As a matter of fact, this consensus already exists. What needs to be done is how to design it and how to translate the consensus into action and establish the EAFTA early.

1. *Policy setting one: How to do it?*

Option One: To negotiate EAFTA on the basis of three "10+1" FTAs, i.e. China–ASEAN FTA, Japan–ASEAN FTA and ROK–ASEAN FTA. The three FTAs will set the basic structure, principles and contents for an EAFTA, and the major issues relating to EAFTA will be settled by three separate FTAs. It means that the modality of the future EAFTA will be a combination of three FTAs. This may be the most feasible approach for establishing the EAFTA.

Option Two: To negotiate EAFTA on the basis of three "10+1" FTAs and Northeast Asian FTA (NAFTA, China–Japan–ROK FTA). Since the three "10+1" FTAs would be realized in a matter of time, NAFTA is key. Currently, Japan–ROK FTA is still under negotiation and expected to be concluded by the end of 2005. The essential part is China's involvement. China has shown its interest in the trilateral FTA process. But Japan does not seem to give a FTA with China (either bilateral or trilateral) priority even though the trilateral study group has done a lot on the feasibility study for a NAFTA. The difficulty is the long wait for NAFTA to be completed if the three countries fail to agree on an early initiative, and EAFTA will be delayed indefinitely if it must proceed only after NAFTA. This option apparently requires more active work from the three Northeast Asian countries.

2. Policy setting two: Who are the members?

East Asian cooperation started from TPT so it should from the core of EAFTA; its role is crucial for success. Considering the fact of the multi-layered FTAs in the region, EAFTA should be established to unify the separate elements into an integrated framework, although newly-defined negotiation is needed.

For its, geographical extension, the first consideration is how to bring two vibrant economies in East Asia, i.e. Hong Kong and Taiwan, into the EAFTA framework. Hong Kong is a free economy. Its participation should not be difficult. Taiwan's participation needs the supports of the rights political environment, i.e. improvement of the Taiwan Straits relations under the "One China" principle. Among other East Asian members, Mongolian participation seems to be just a matter of time so long as Mongolia itself is ready.

The linkage between EAFTA and CER could be considered in two ways: one is to encourage Australia and New Zealand to join EAFTA through separate negotiation after the conclusion of the EAFTA negotiation, while another is to integrate the two FTAs. The question for the first approach is that both countries do not belong to the East Asian region. EAFTA has to be renamed if the two could be admitted. The difficulty of the second approach is that it has to wait until EAFTA is completed.

India is active in developing economic cooperation with ASEAN and other East Asian countries. It has shown strong interest in participating in EAFTA and has called on the developing of the Asian FTA (also Asian Community). Considering that the scope of an Asian FTA is too big to be clearly defined, one should be cautious to extend EAFTA into an Asian FTA even in the mid-term. Indian participation in the EAFTA should be specifically defined and handled.

3. *Policy setting three: What model should be followed?*

Considering the economic development level of ASEAN and China, CAFTA may be a feasible model for the future EAFTA which is characterized by a gradual approach: liberalization of trade for goods first followed by investment and services; more developed economies moving faster, and less developed economies, slower; liberalization of competitive sectors first, sensitive sectors later. Until 2010, the majority of trade in goods (85 percent) will be liberalized (zero tariff). As a matter of fact, CAFTA is a kind of CEP since it covers wide areas of liberation, facilitation and cooperation.

As mentioned above, since the best approach towards EAFTA may be a combination of three "10+1" FTAs, it is appropriate to negotiate a comprehensive EAFTA based on these. With three ready "10+1" FTAs, all difficult problems, like liberalization of the agriculture sector, labor mobility, rule of origin, as well as special treatment of less developed countries, would be settled in a separate agreement. EAFTA would actually restructure the three agreements into an integrated one.

Based on the above policy settings, a road map for EAFTA is taking shape:

With "10+3" as the core, ASEAN and the three Northeast Asian countries together lead the way towards an EAFTA and gradually extend it to new members.

If the three "10+1" FTA is the foundation, the time-table to negotiate a "1+3"-based EAFTA is after 2007 when negotiation of all three FTAs would be concluded. It is desirable to conclude the negotiation of EAFTA by 2010 and have it established before 2020.[6]

China and Japan should cooperate closely in establishing EAFTA and EAC in general. The two countries have two choices: one is to launch the EAFTA negotiation directly based on the three "10+1"

---

[6] We are considering two important events in setting this time table: one is the ASEAN Economic Community, another is the APEC Bogor goal for trade and investment liberalization in the Asia-Pacific.

FTAs, while another is to complete the bilateral (China–Japan) or the trilateral (China–Japan–ROK) FTA early (before 2008).

EAFTA is a key part of East Asian community-building (EAC). Its success is of great significance to the progress of the cooperation in other areas and EAC as a whole. Of course, considering the diversity of East Asia, the implementation of EAFTA will be gradual, and social as well as political factors should be taken into serious consideration.

CHAPTER NINE

How to Promote Monetary and Financial Cooperation in East Asia[1]

Under the "10+3" cooperation framework, East Asian monetary and financial cooperation has gained some progress. The major visible achievement is the Chiang Mai Initiative (CMI), i.e. the money swap arrangements between central banks. Now, it is necessary to make clear the directions and goals for further East Asian cooperation.

The cooperation among East Asian central banks and finance ministries is not merely financial cooperation in the ordinary sense. It also includes monetary cooperation, regional coordination in the area of monetary policy and exchange rate policy. The current money swap arrangements are aimed at financial rescue to prevent a new financial crisis. They can also be viewed as monetary cooperation aiming at stabilizing currencies.

In general, the immediate goal for East Asian monetary and financial cooperation is to stabilize the regional financial market through strengthening regional capacity to counter financial shocks, thus avoiding the recurrence of a financial crisis in the East Asia region. This plays an important role in promoting sustained and stable economic growth in the region.

---

[1] This is a policy report written for the Trilateral Financial Cooperation Dialogue between China, Japan and South Korea in March 2003.

I. A Step Further

One significant progress in East Asian monetary and financial cooperation is consensus-building on the necessity of strengthening regional monetary and financial cooperation. The Chiang Mai Initiative (CMI) has set up a stable foundation for East Asia monetary and financial cooperation.

East Asia still faces two kinds of risks: exchange risk and debt risk. There are differences and connections between these two risks. The exchange risk can be the result of the debt risk, and vice versa. Thus, it can be said that actions and goals to prevent these two risks are identical.

Because financial crisis tends to be contagious in nature, the short-term goal for East Asian countries is to strengthen both independent and collective capacity to counter currency crisis and to avoid the recurrence of a financial crisis. To achieve this, the immediate agenda is how to improve both the mechanism-building and the capacity-building.

After the East Asian financial crisis, Japan put forward a proposal for an Asian monetary fund. But it was premature. Instead, in May 2000, at the annual ADB meeting held at Chiang Mai, Thailand, East Asian countries agreed to establish a network of bilateral money swap arrangements between central banks to counter any possible financial crisis and protect currencies under speculative attack.

The Chiang Mai Initiative and the subsequent money swap agreements can be considered as a regional self-rescue mechanism and a complement to the present IMF rescue mechanisms. It is a practical choice based on the existing political and economic conditions in East Asia. However, compared with the Asian monetary fund, the CMI embodies many elements of symbols and the money swap arrangements are small in size. The rescue pattern is on a bilateral basis, not a multi-lateral one. It is essential that the size of monetary swaps be increased and a cooperative management mechanism at a regional level be established. Accordingly, the current main task is to further perfect the mechanisms on the basis of the CMI.

How do we move ahead from current progress? We should set up guiding rules, accomplish a transition from a bilateral mechanism to a regional mechanism, and enlarge the size of monetary swaps.

It is necessary for us to establish guiding rules to standardize and regulate the economic policies and actions of the countries engaged in East Asian cooperation.

Financial rescue through promises of monetary swap is a "post response" or "passive action". This means that others have to take responsibility for their counterpart's problem since any financial crisis has a serious effect of contagion. The swap arrangement is considered a mechanism of mutual and reciprocal responsibility. However, this embodies the risk of undertake responsibility for having to counterpart's a mistake. Therefore, there should be some restraint on the counterpart's actions to prevent mistakes as much as possible. Accordingly guiding rules are necessary for economic behavior and indicators of macroeconomic performance. It goes without saying that how to implement the rules and how to make them effective remain a complex problem. They must be related to regional macroeconomic dialogues and cooperation. Nevertheless, financial cooperation should obviously more faster than overall macroeconomic cooperation.

At present, monetary swap arrangements between larger countries have been finalized. But the overall size of the swaps remains too small. If it is a monetary swap arrangement at the regional level, the size should be expanded to at least US$80 billion. So far, total foreign exchange reserves of East Asian economies have exceeded US$1,000 billion. It should not be a problem to enlarge the scale of money swap arrangements (or other forms of financing arrangements).

There are two ways to enlarge the scale of money swaps. One is a simple increase. For instance, the scale of monetary swap can be doubled from the existing amount. This seems simple and might not be in accord with the economic strength of each country. The other way is to fix money swap agreements according to the GDP of each country. Large economic powers in East Asia such as Japan,

China, and the NIEs have much more influence in the region and must undertake more regional responsibility.

The use of swap money, must be based on IMF principles (for instance, terms and procedures of loans), thereby preventing any possible financing risk. Financing risk is reciprocal and two-way. If the swap arrangement works well, it may be a good start to transform the regional swap to a regional monetary fund.

In order to manage the regional swap fund, the establishment of some mechanisms for East Asian monetary cooperation should be considered, such as formulation of articles of management and formation of a committee for monetary cooperation appropriate to East Asian conditions.

At the same time, we need to further explore and improve the mechanisms of economic reviews and macroeconomic policy coordination under the "10+3" framework. It is also necessary to establish early warning indicators and a system in preparation for crisis. The macroeconomic policies that need coordination include fiscal policy, monetary policy and exchange rate policy. Among them, the exchange rate policy is the most important and difficult. In order to avoid big fluctuations of exchange rates, it is important to prevent competitive currency devaluation and to reduce mistakes in macroeconomic policies that might lead to a financial crisis. Macroeconomic policy coordination can also be done through mechanisms for peer review and peer monitoring.

In October 1998, ASEAN finance ministers signed the Terms of Understanding that established the ASEAN Surveillance Process. According to the principles of peer review and mutual interest among ASEAN countries (ASP), the overall purpose of the ASP is to strengthen policymaking capacity within ASEAN. ASP is still an important development for ASEAN economic and monetary integration. It is necessary to consider how to make ASP work and apply it to the East Asian region within the 10+3 framework. At present, an ASEAN+3 Surveillance Process is taking shape. The first peer review meeting was held along with the ADB annual meeting in May 2000. However, owing to the huge difference in the level of economic development in the region, there exists great difficulty in coordinating macroeconomic policies of the countries. Therefore, the present mechanisms for macroeconomic policy coordination in East Asia seem to be preliminary.

To strengthen East Asian monetary and financial cooperation, we need to establish a relatively sound macroeconomic information exchange system which can serve as the basis for macroeconomic policy coordination. Information exchange is an important step in the ASEAN Surveillance Process, the ASEAN+3 Surveillance Process and the CMI. It includes mainly information about capital flows and leading domestic economic indicators. Central banks and finance ministries must be in consultations concerning monetary and financial cooperation, financial regulation, information exchange, etc.

Some progress have been achieved in the cooperation of strengthening capability-building. However, it is far from enough. East Asian countries might consider the establishment of a specialized institution and a special fund (something like APEC finance and development project) to strengthen personnel training and personnel exchange. In the meantime, East Asian countries should cooperate with IMF, European Central Bank, BIS and ADB in personnel training and personnel exchange. Research projects and programs concerning East Asian monetary and financial cooperation should also be considered.

II. A Longer-term View

The goal for East Asian monetary and financial cooperation is to further improve regional self-financing capacity and establish a mature mechanism for crisis prevention. If the US dollar fluctuates sharply relative to the Japanese Yen or Euro, East Asian countries will face great exchange rate risk which would have a negative impact on their trade and economy. To pre-empt this, East Asia needs to stabilize the mechanisms for monetary cooperation, expand their scope and deepen regional cooperation.

Since East Asian central banks have concluded their money swap agreements, every country in the region should undertake responsibility for maintaining the stability of the exchange rate. Accordingly, an explicit agreement is needed to restrain each country's conduct. The prevention of undue fluctuations of exchange rates is an essential goal for East Asian monetary cooperation.

So far, there have been many discussions about regional cooperation in stabilizing exchange rates. There is a general understanding that, each country should stabilize the exchange rate of its own currency. Then, a mechanism for regional consultation and dialogue should be established to prevent any financial crisis. Through regional cooperation, there will be interventions and rescues when a crisis occurs. The establishment of an exchange rate mechanism like the European one is complicated and many conditions are needed. If we take the exchange rate mechanism as one of the main points of cooperation within the "10+3" framework, we have to try to set up some non-binding guidelines and be committed to self-restraint. A possible arrangement is to introduce a flexible ban for the exchange rate fluctuation for each currency. This ban can only be consideration for; not a commitment, or a responsibility, i.e. it is a non-binding guideline. Japan and China should undertake more responsibility to stabilize exchange rates and avoid competitive currency devaluation. If this works, this kind of coordination mechanism for exchange rate policy may be progressively transferred to a formal and binding East Asia exchange rate mechanism.

For a long-term goal, one possibility for an East Asia exchange rate mechanism is to adopt the common basket peg and create a regional currency unit that can be used for trade accounting and also a possible means of payment within the region. Currencies in the region might be mutually pegged internally and commonly pegged externally. Nevertheless, many difficulties must be overcome which will depend on the overall East Asian cooperation process. A currency unit needs high political consolidation and a high-level of regional integration, which, in East Asia, seems to need a very long time.

The establishment of an Asian monetary fund is a feasible way to promote East Asian monetary cooperation. The basic functions of the fund are to stabilize regional currencies, to prevent and counter any financial crisis and to serve as a complement to the IMF. An Asian monetary fund will have a deterrent effect on speculative capital, intervense in markets, and provide emergency rescue of member countries. The Asian Monetary Fund should monitor and supervise economic development, economic structure, financial markets and economic policies of member countries. A regional consultation mechanism will be established for study and research, and information on macroeconomic performance, economic policy and financial markets exchanged. By exerting pressure on member countries, the fund will prevent member countries from implementing policies that might lead to a financial crisis.

III. Beyond Monetary Cooperation

The Asian financial crisis has proved that, if there are no common institutional frameworks in East Asia, the region is incapable of countering any crisis. In the European Union, member countries have made great efforts to strengthen institution-building in order to integrate the market.

Accordingly, East Asia should set up some preliminary form of regional cooperation institution if the region is to achieve high-level integration. Institutionalization of East Asian cooperation will mean establishing a coordination office, a secretariat, or a kind of formal organization. Task forces for monetary and financial cooperation, trade, regional development and environment should also be set up as affiliates. This might be an embryonic form for a future formal East Asian organization. At present, the establishment of a secretariat for East Asian cooperation is on the agenda of East Asian leaders. As a first step, it might be better to establish an independent secretariat within the "10+3" framework. If this is difficult to achieve, expanding the work scope of the ASEAN Secretariat under the "10+3" framework could be considered. China, Japan and Korea may send their representatives to the

Secretariat. In this way, the ASEAN Secretariat will expand its work scope to coordinate the whole of East Asian cooperation.

We also need to strengthen East Asian political dialogue and cooperation. In addition to economic factors, a strong political will among East Asian countries is necessary for East Asian monetary and financial cooperation. East Asian economic cooperation is both an economic and political process. Macroeconomic policy coordination and peer review mechanism involve the issue of state economic sovereignty. At present, the political foundation is too weak for East Asian economic cooperation. There exist great diversity in the political, economic, cultural and historical dimensions among East Asian countries. Monetary and financial cooperation must overcome each country's strong sense of state sovereignty. Therefore, along with the development of economic globalization, East Asian countries must develop a more open and flexible concept of state sovereignty. The East Asian financial crisis has forced East Asian countries to face up to the importance of cooperation. The political will for cooperation among East Asian countries is becoming stronger. However, considering the existing economic and political obstacles, East Asian monetary integration can only be a gradual process.

China has emerged to become an important stabilizing factor for East Asia. China will naturally play a key role in East Asian economic development and cooperation. At the end of 2002, China and ASEAN concluded a series of political and economic agreements. The establishment of a comprehensive cooperation partnership has shown that mutual political trust and economic cooperation between China and ASEAN have advanced to a mature stage. China, operating on the principle of peace and development, is the most positive factor for East Asian cooperation.

The actual development of East Asian monetary and financial cooperation will depend on the overall economic cooperation and development in the region. East Asian economy is presently undergoing an important adjustment. Economic interdependence among East Asian countries is deepening. Advancement of East Asian economic integration will certainly be beneficial to East Asian cooperation. East Asian economies will quicken their pace for economic and trade cooperation which may help to lead to an early establishment of the East Asian free trade area. Any regional trade area can serve in a complementary role to WTO. This will in turn be beneficial to East Asian economic integration and help to narrow the gaps of economic development among East Asian countries. In the long run, it will help to promote East Asian monetary and financial cooperation to an advanced level.

At the moment, positive developments can be seen in the establishment of multilateral and bilateral free trade areas in East Asia. The ASEAN free trade area has been basically established. The China–ASEAN free trade area will be set up within 10 years. Japan and Singapore signed a bilateral free trade agreement. A proposal for China–Japan–Korea free trade area is now under study. All these free trade agreements will be conducive to establishment of a free trade area covering the whole of East Asia.

Gradualism and convergence are valuable lessons from European monetary integration. In a broad sense, monetary integration is an advanced form of economic integration. Economic integration involves coordination and concordance of economic policies and mutual surveillance by concerned countries. This implies the surrender to some extent of state sovereignty to the regional institution. Monetary union requires a country to abandon a certain degree of its monetary sovereignty and independence. Full monetary union requires a country to abandon its national currency and implement monetary policy set by a super-national central bank and to be subject to the supervision by a super-national institution. Through a process of gradualism and convergence, European countries formed the European Monetary and Economic Union. The situation in East Asia seems much more complicated than that in Europe. The monetary integration in East Asia might need a much longer process of gradualism and convergence than Europe.

References

Jackson, K. D. (1999). *Asian contagion: The causes and consequences of a financial crisis.* Westview Press.

Kaufman, G. G., T. H. Krueger and W. C. Hunter (1999). *The Asian Financial Crisis: Origins, Implications and Solutions*. Springer.

Palma, G. (2000). *The Three Routes to Financial Crises: The Need for Capital Controls*. Cambridge University, Center for Economic Policy Analysis.

Pempel, T. J. (1999). *The Politics of the Asian Economic Crisis*. Ithaca, NY: Cornell University Press.

Radelet, S., J. D. Sachs, R. N. Cooper and B. P. Bosworth (1998). *The East Asian Financial Crisis: Diagnosis, Remedies, Prospects*. Brookings Papers on Economic Activity.

Stiglitz, J. (1996). *Some Lessons from the East Asian Miracle*. The World Bank: Research Observer.

Wang, X. (2003). Pondering after Asian Financial Crisis. *Financial Studies*, 2. www.periodical.ilib.cn

Wu, X. (2002). Deeper Reasons Inducing Asian Financial Crisis. *Commercial Research*, 1.

CHAPTER TEN

The Asian Financial Crisis and Regional Cooperation[1]

Introduction

Eost Asia is experiencing its worst economic crisis resulting from the financial crisis that started Thailand in July of 1997. The crisis is so serious that it has expanded to many other parts of the world. The concern is when the financial market could return to normal and economies could recover.

The main work for policy-makers now is how to prevent a crash of the international financial market leading to a world-wide economic recession. This urgency is recognized by the international community, especially by the leaders of East Asia.

Why is the East Asian region suddenly plunged into such difficulty? Only about a year ago before the financial crisis, East Asia was still considered as the center of world economic growth and the future of the forthcoming "Asian Century." Now it has become the source of the crisis and a region of increasing pessimism. As one commentator pointed out, "The downturn has been so deep and the currency deprecations so large in Asian's crisis-struck economies that regaining the lost ground will take several years."[2]

---

[1] This paper was written in 1998 for the conference on East Asian Economic Outlook organized by Institute of South East Asian Studies, Singapore in December, 1998.
[2] G. Pierre Goad (19 October 1998). "Asia mulls scope of rebound from its economic turmoil". *The Asian Wall Street Journal*.

What went wrong? There seems no simple answer since the crisis is a long-term accumulation of problems on one hand, and a changed market environment on the other.

China has avoided a financial crisis, and its economy is still going strong in 1998 and possibly in the next few years. China has become an important factor for the stability of the regional economy.

However, China cannot be playing alone. The negative effects of the financial crisis are profound and long-term. The IMF intervention has proved not very helpful to the crisis-affected economies. What we need is urgent regional cooperation to prevent further contagion of the crisis and to help the economies recover as early as possible.

I. The Root of the Financial Crisis

The East Asian crisis has dramatically changed perceptions about the region. The regional economies used to be overwhelmed by views of its past success as miraculous and seemingly bright future as a center of the "new Asian century." But with the crisis, pessimism is prevailing.

The debate on " miracle or myth" for the East Asian economies in the past two decades has been revived. No matter how controversial, the economic miracle of East Asia is real. In the past two decades, the East Asian region experienced much faster growth than any other region in the world, which increased its share in the world GDP from less than one tenth in early 1970s to a quarter in the mid-1990s. The increase in per capita income in Republic of Korea (South Korea) is as large as tenfold, fivefold in Thailand, fourfold in Malaysia, close to fivefold in China.[3] However, what is surprising is why after such a long period of success did the economies of East Asia suddenly find themselves floundering?

---

[3] For China, the figure is per capita GDP, from late 1970s to late 1990s. *A Statistical Survey of China*, 1998, p. 15, China Statistical Publisher. For the other figures, see *Asia Society: Asia at a Crossroads*, 1998, p. 11.

The causes

There is no simple answer for the causes of the financial crisis since it is the result of many accumulated factors. Even if the major factor lies in the inherent problems of the Asian economies, the role of outside factors should not be underestimated.

Within the region, a long-term high rate of economic growth caused imbalance. For example, excess capacities existed in almost every country. As a result, the prices of manufactured goods came down sharply, starting from early 1996 in many countries. The increasing losses of banks and businesses shook market stability and confidence even though "the fundamentals" (high savings rate, prudent fiscal and monetary policies etc.) of the economies were still good.

At the same time, sustained expansionary policies to support high economic growth caused imprudent lending and borrowing, especially borrowing from abroad. In the 1990s, short-term foreign borrowing in some Asian countries increased very rapidly, which exacerbated their foreign debt. Furthermore, the prevailing optimistic expectation about the future then and the pegged exchange rates allowed too much short-term capital flow into the region, which made the debt structure even more vulnerable and the economies unsustainable (see Tables 1 and 2).

As estimated, as much as US$100 billion flowed into South East Asia every year after the mid-1990s. Too much capital (especially short-term loans and portfolio investment) was seeking short-term profit. This is very risky once uncertainty emerges. A weak financial

Table 1: Debt structure of Asian countries in crisis (%).

	Korea	Indonesia	Thailand
Short-term Debt	68	59	65.7
Debt/GDP	25	37	46
Debt/FE reserve	350	190	180

Source: *Economist*, 18 March 1998, p. 10.
Note: FE reserve-foreign exchange reserve.

Table 2: Short term debt of Asian countries in crisis (%).

	1990	1994	1997
S-t Debt/FR			
Korea	115	165	211
Thailand	54	101	148
Indonesia	–	177	174
S-t Debt/GDP			
Korea	7	9	16
Thailand	7	19	17
Indonesia	–	11	17

Source: *Asia: Responding to crisis*, ADB Institute, 1998, p. 10.
Note: FR = foreign exchange reserve, S-t Debt = short-term debt.

sector together with the quick liberalization of the capital markets makes the financial market unstable. In fact, all crisis-hit economies lack efficient financial instruments to manage and regulate the market. Before the crisis, most of the governments in the region focused largely on facilitating capital inflow, rather than on supervising and controlling the problems. As a result, irresponsible lending and borrowing were almost unchecked. In a liberalized financial market, together with new high-tech international financial instruments, hedge funds can move in and out very quickly and massively. This becomes an important source of disturbances which, in highly integrated financial markets, can be easily transmitted from one country to another. The panic not only stopped capital inflow, but also triggered net outflow. In fact, there were dramatic capital outflows from the East Asian region after the crisis started in July of 1997.

The deterioration of the Japanese economy and weakened financial sector made the crisis even worse. Japan, the largest economy in East Asia and also the largest lender and investor in the region, should have played a positive role in helping the region out of the crisis, but instead became "a falling goose." Japan's long economic recession, sharp depreciation of the Yen, decreasing imports, and, especially, the poorly managed banking sector with mounting bad loans — all greatly worsened the situation. Besides, a slow reaction to the crisis by the US government and "improper medicine" to crisis-hit countries by the IMF (focusing on austerity rather than on recovery) created some counter-productive effects to the stability and recovery of the regional economy.

East Asia has never experienced a crisis in such scope and depth. It is viewed quite differently by each crisis-hit country with their different problems and economic structures. Although it is neither a crisis of the "Asian model" or "Asian values," the contagion reflects the fact that the region and the world as a whole has become highly integrated and interdependent.

The lessons

The financial crisis has caused sharp contraction in the economic activities of the region. The economies of Indonesia, Korea, Thailand, as well as Japan, will again have negative growth rates in 1998. Economic recession, together with structural readjustments and reforms, has also brought about painful social costs. There are lessons to draw from this crisis.

It is evident that healthy economic development must be based on a balance of efficient input and output. A sustained expansionary macro-economic policy focusing on continuous high growth results in structural imbalance — overheating the market with excess capacity, over-valued equity price and risky stock market etc. It is now recognized that an average 8–10 percent annual growth for a decade or two may create serious imbalance. The East Asian countries should craft their economic policies for balanced and stable growth, especially considering changes in the regional and international market structure and environment in the future.

The facts show that market liberalization and high-tech international financial system enable quick and easy capital flow. Nevertheless, the massive capital inflow, if mostly of short-term capital, either through borrowing or investments, results in a high risk of market destruction. Speculation by hedge funds may cause a sudden crash of the financial market, and the subsequent outward rush of investments only leads to a destruction of the stock market. The host country must find a way to control short-term capital flow, especially hedge funds, and of course, at the same time to build up a strong and efficient banking sector together with effective supervision instruments. At the same time, the international financial system needs to be reformed to meet the new challenges.

At present, what is most worrying is not just the pervasive nature of the financial and economic crisis in the East Asian region, but also a danger of further contagion to the other parts of the world — a global crisis. The regional as well as international communities should act collectively and firmly to build up confidence and take effective measures to restore the foundation of economic recovery.[4]

II. How did China Avoid the Crisis?

The Chinese economy has avoided the financial crisis. It has kept a stable exchange rate of the Yuan and strong economic growth. Why is China different?

An early cooling down

The Chinese economy has kept up with a high growth rate since the 1980s. The average growth rate was 9.5 percent in the 1980s, 9.5 percent in the first half of the 1990s. However, the growth of the economy in the 1990s was not smooth. A recession began in 1989, but the economy started to recover from 1991, with the growth rate up from 3.8 percent in 1990 to 9.2 percent in 1991. It started to heat from 1992, with double digit inflation and GDP growth.

The Chinese government has adopted timely measures to cool down the economy since 1993 through controlling bank lending, restructuring bad loans etc. The economy realized a "soft landing" by the end of 1996, with its growth rate coming down

---

[4] C. Fred Bergsten proposed that a concerted Asian recovery program should be launched at the summit of the Asia-Pacific Economic Cooperation (APEC) in Kuala Lumpur in November this year. *Asia Week*, 8 October 1998, p. 73.

under 10 percent, and further down to 8.8 percent in 1997, and inflation dropping out of sight since the middle of the year. As Peter Botttelier, now senior advisor to World Bank, commented: "If China had not made the difficult internal policy and institutional adjustments that permitted a "soft landing" in 1996, the Asian financial crisis would probably have dragged the economy in a much more serious way."[5]

No debt crisis

China has benefited largely from her open policy in realizing a long-term and stable high economic growth. China is the largest recipient of foreign investment among the developing countries, and the second largest in foreign direct investment (FDI) in the world after the United States. However, China has kept a healthy structure of capital inflow since long-term debt accounts for the larger proportion (more than 80 percent) and FDI plays the major role (see Figure 1). There is no real danger of a debt crisis

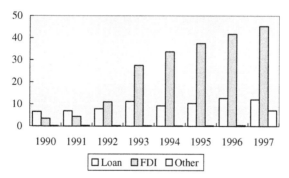

Source: A Statistical Survey of China, 1998.

Figure 1:   Structure of foreign capital flow (in billion US dollars).

---

[5] See David Shambaugh (ed.) (1998). *Is China Unstable?* George Washington University, p. 57.

though China has received increasing amounts of foreign capital. Importantly, China has adopted a gradual approach in opening her financial market. China had not made her currency quickly convertible. The current account was opened in 1996, but capital market liberalization is still in the process of preparation. This made it impossible for speculators to attack the Chinese currency. In considering the aftermath of the Asian financial crisis, it seems that a cautious transition towards full liberalization of the financial market is necessary, especially for developing countries.

Foreign trade has played a very important role in the Chinese economy. China is now the 10th largest country in the world. A high growth of exports has made the Chinese economy dynamic; for example, the contribution from exports to GDP is close to 20 percent in 1997. Increasing trade surplus in the 1990s especially enabled China to build up the capacity to pay back its foreign debt with increasing foreign exchange reserves (over US$140 billion by the end of 1997). Compared with countries suffering from the debt crisis, China had a much healthier foreign trade balance in the mid-1990s (see Figure 2).

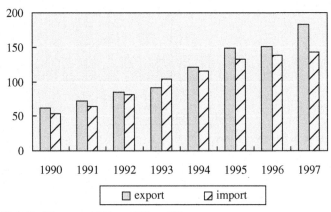

Source: A Statistical Survey of China, 1998, p. 133.

Figure 2:   The balance of China's import and export in 1990s (in billion US dollars).

Effective measures

From 1993, the Chinese government took effective steps to control over lending. Emergency measures were adopted after July 1997 during the Asia financial crisis. These included:

— Closing some irresponsible banks and credit units;
— Increasing capital-debt ratio of major state banks (to 8 percent);
— Re-centralizing the control of foreign borrowing.
— Setting up a special fund for domestic bad loans (30 billion Yuan starting from 1994, with 10 billion added annually);
— Strengthening the evaluation and monitoring of listed companies.

However, to some extent, the debt problem (bad loans) is still worrisome. As a result of the earlier bubble economy, as well as eventual effect of the financial crisis, some problems have become apparent. For example, some banks or investment and trust companies are in trouble. A more recent case is the closure of Guangdong International Investment and Trust Company (Gitic), which has a big amount of bad loans both on the domestic and the foreign markets.

Yuan is stable

Amidst the devaluation of major currencies in the region, the exchange rate of the Chinese currency, the Yuan, is still stable. The Chinese government has stated again and again that it has no intention to devalue the Yuan. How has the exchange rate of the Yuan be kept stable?

The Chinese currency huge has experienced fluctuations during economic reform and development, but it became stable after 1994 when it moved to a unified market rate (see Figure 3). The current rate is considered to be reasonable.

The fundamentals for the stability of Yuan are there. Domestically its current account or foreign debt is in a healthy state. A high foreign exchange reserve (more than US$140 billion by the end of the third quarter of 1998) and reasonable foreign debt ratio (about 15 percent of GDP) provide a firm base for the market.

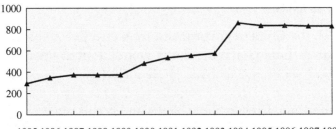

Source: A Statistical Survey of China, 1998, p. 134.

Note: For 1998, the rate is mid-August; for the other years, the yearly-based middle rate.

Figure 3:   Exchange Rate of Yuan (to US$, yearly based, mid-level).

Although exports are less dynamic with growth rate of only 3.9 percent in the first nine months of 1998, the trade balance is still positive with 15 percent increase of trade surplus to US$35.3 billion in the same period.[6] It is clear that market confidence in the Chinese currency is still keeping firm.

Within the region a competitive devaluation of the currencies only makes the crisis worse since the major challenge to Chinese exports is the decline in demand from its trade partners due to their financial and economic crisis.

Besides, unlike the other East Asian countries in crisis, the Chinese capital market has not been fully opened which makes it difficult for hedge funds to speculate on the foreign exchange market in China. A cautious liberalization policy on the financial market provides more room for the Chinese government to manage the crisis.

Generally speaking, the Chinese economy has benefited from a stable currency which keeps costs low since imported parts account for a very high proportion in exported goods. However, the real challenge of the devaluation of other currencies to China has been recognized. China may loose the competitive edge in many export goods, if the other currencies continue to be at a very low rate. It is reasonable to keep the Chinese Yuan on a stable base,

---

[6] *Economic Daily* (Beijing), 13 October 1998.

but not necessarily at a fixed rate, even if there is no pressure for devaluation in the immediate future.

The Chinese economy would continue to grow in a good environment if there were no Asia financial crisis. With successful readjustment of the economy during 1993–1997, the new government headed by Zhu Rongji decided to speed up reforms on state-owned enterprises (SOEs) in 1998. Unfortunately, the financial crisis has brought about a negative environment for reform and economic growth. The main concern for the Chinese government is how to prevent the economy from sliding. The government has made great efforts to keep its growth target of eight percent for 1998. The significance of this lies in the governments ability to create employment with a high growth rate.

It is a big challenge for Chinese economy to grow at such a high rate in the face of an economic slowdown in the Asia-Pacific and in the world as a whole. The growth rate is only seven percent in the first half of 1998. The industrial growth is well below target, only 7.9 percent. The major problem is that demand is rather weak due to a slowdown of domestic consumption and exports.

Special measures have been taken in order to grow the economy at a reasonable rate. The government has decided to increase expenditure in the investment of infrastructure. There are as large as 200 billion Yuan investments in infrastructure projects ranging from highways and railways to environment protection through issuing of special government bonds and corresponding bank credit starting from the third quarter of 1998. This is expected to add 1.5 percentage to 2 percentages of GDP growth. Compared with the growth structure in 1997, domestic investment will have to contribute at least one percentage more to GDP. Data of the third quarter shows that GDP growth has rebounded to 7.6 percent, supported by high growth of domestic investment (28.2 percent) and the rebounding of industrial production (10.2 percent), though exports have declined, down to −2.2 percent.

It is wise to keep the economy growing through increased domestic expenditure since external demand is weak. However, what is worrisome is that this government-led expenditure may hide the real structural problems of the economy, for example, the inefficiency of the investments which has existed for quite some time. In fact, the Chinese banking system is still very fragile since there is a high debt to equity ratio of Chinese companies on the one hand, and high ratio of non-performing loans on the other hand. Fortunately, the Asian crisis has added a new sense of urgency for the Chinese leaders to introduce further reform, especially with regards to the SOEs and the financial system. Chinese economic development cannot be sustained without high efficiency of investment and production.

III. Calling for Regional Cooperation

It is important to understand that the Chinese economy is not sustainable if the regional economies will not recover soon. The financial crisis has shown that the quick contagion is partly a result of failed consolidation of the countries in the region. The IMF's rescue fund is helpful, but its intervention seems harmful. What is surprising is the very slow reaction by the United States. What's very urgent is to encourage cooperation in the East Asian region.

What can be done? One option is to create an emergency fund to support the crisis-hit economies. Japan may be affected, but Japan has the ability to play a major role to provide funds to other affected economies. China should play an active role in assisting the affected countries as its stability is greatly helpful to the region.

However, what is more necessary is for the region to strengthen cooperation to overcome difficulties and recover market confidence which is essential for economic recovery. There are several things that should be done now:

(1) High-level consultation and coordination with the participation of all regional economies, for example, via financial ministers' meeting or even a summit meeting.
(2) Emergency macroeconomic discussion and cooperation on economic policies, including financial and monetary policies.

(3) Enhancing financial supervision and improvement in order to rescue banks and other financial institutions.

(4) Promoting regional financial mechanism in the financial sector and other sectors. Some kind of regional financial facility is necessary, not just for the current crisis, but also for future regional development.

(5) Promoting regional trade and investment liberalization to avoid protectionalism since East Asian economies have benefited from liberalization of the markets.

The financial crisis has greatly damaged East Asia's economic growth. Great efforts are needed to put the regional economies back on the normal track. We should have confidence for the future. The miracle of the past may have ended but the future has just begun.

CHAPTER ELEVEN

Environment and Energy Cooperation in East Asia[1]

I. Environment and Energy Challenges

East Asia is facing the challenges of continuing environmental degradation, unhealthy air and water conditions, escalating demands for energy and other resource inputs and increasing certainty that climate change and other global environmental problems will have substantial negative impacts upon the region. Especially in the developing economies, the cost to the environment has been increasing that does not just threaten the potential of economic growth, but finally the sustainability of economic development.

Thus, environmental problems have become a priority concern for the regional and global community since it can directly affect the efficiency of resource investments and the eventual achievement of development objectives.[2]

The environment and energy are closely related. The continuing and accelerating emissions of greenhouse gas (GHG), and its close link to rising global temperatures, are likely to result in significant

---

[1] This is the report to the expert group for feasibility study on CEPEA (close economic partnership for East Asia) in 2008.
[2] Simone Gigli and Shardul Agrawala (2007). Stocking of progress on integrating adaptation to Climate Change into Development Co-operation Activities, OECD.

changes in climate and its intra-seasonal and inter-annual variability, both globally and in Asia.[3]

Energy demand is increasing rapidly due to the unprecedented economic growth in the region. In developing Asia, fossil fuels will remain a dominant source of energy — accounting for over 84 percent of the overall increase in global demand between 2005 and 2030. Because of its high dependence on fossil fuels, Asia now accounts for 27 percent of the world's energy-related GHG emissions, three times its share 30 years ago. Therefore, the foundation of sustainable development is to make economies as energy-efficient as possible.[4]

With better understanding of this phenomenon, countries have increasingly adopted policies to reduce the projected energy demand; however, much more needs to be done to reverse the current trend of GHG emissions. With high energy prices and fierce competition for energy supply, it is important to develop alternative new energy sources and to adopt new technology that would lead to more efficient and clean energy consumption in helping to reduce GHG. This needs close cooperation in the regional as well as global level.

Efforts must be made to meet essential energy needs through low-carbon and zero-carbon options. Incremental costs for biomass co-generation, wind, geothermal, hydropower and solar water heating are fast declining, and in many areas with rich renewable resources, these options are becoming competitive against the cost of using fossil fuels. Thus, demand- and supply-side interventions must go hand in hand to address carbon emissions from energy consumption.[5] New policies are needed to encourage and support producing and using new forms of energy, and society should be educated for change.

---

[3] ADB (2007). Strategy Paper, Document Stage: Draft for Consultation.
[4] Ursula Schäfer-Preuss (2007). The Challenges of Energy and Environment in Asia. Speech at the *Conference on Multilateral Economic Cooperation with the Association of Southeast Asian Nations* (CMEC–ASEAN), 18 September 2007, Berlin, Germany.
[5] Ursula Schäfer-Preuss (2007). The Challenges of Energy and Environment in Asia.

II. Challenge of Climate Change

Climate change is a common concern of the international community and a hot topic on the international agenda. Global CO_2 emissions are growing faster than at any time since 1970 with the world's strongest economic growth in decades (see Table 1).[6] The current situation offers a serious warning. The atmospheric concentration of carbon dioxide in 2005 has exceeded by far the natural range over the last 650,000 years. The current concentration of GHGs in the atmosphere has led to an increase of global mean temperature by 0.56–0.92°C. If the present speed of emission of greenhouse gases were to continue, it is projected that global mean temperature will rise by 1.1 to 6.4°C and the sea level will rise by 0.09 to 0.88 meters.[7]

Table 1: Carbon dioxide emission.

	CO_2 Emissions US 1000 tons	GDP US$ bn	CO_2 Emission per US$ Mil GDP	CO_2 Emissions per capita
Australia	226,000	890	253.93	10.81
Brunei	1467	13	112.89	3.76
China	2,680,000	3249	824.87	2.03
India	583,000	1090	534.86	0.52
Indonesia	92,900	410	226.59	0.41
Japan	400,000	4346	92.04	3.13
Korea	185,000	950	194.74	3.82
Malaysia	61,100	165	370.73	2.28
New Zealand	10,600	124	85.48	2.53
Philippines	35,900	141	254.61	0.40
Singapore	20,600	153	134.64	4.59
Thailand	76,400	226	338.05	1.15
Vietnam	28,500	69	413.04	0.33

Source: IMF World Economic Outlook, October 2007, PECC: State of the Region, 2007–2008.

[6] Robert W. Bacon and Soma Bhattacharya (2007). Growth and CO2 Emissions How Do Different Countries Fare? World Bank Working Paper 113.
[7] Sun Guoshun (2007). Climate change and China's position. *Foreign Affairs Journal*, 85.

Climate change leads to serious problems on earth. It may cause the melting of ice caps and snow cover in the polar areas and on high mountains, and result in the rising of the sea level and affecting billions of people living near the sea or in low-lying areas. Climate change may aggravate extreme weather conditions, such as floods, droughts, hurricanes, etc. which lead to more damage to the world. Climate change may cause health problems or lead to the spread of diseases. It may also affect the natural ecosystem, food safety, sustainable development and even the existence of human society.

Climate change must be addressed by the international community through coordination and cooperation. No single country or a group of countries is capable of addressing a global issue of such magnitude. Climate change was addressed in the early 1970s by the UN, and real efforts have been made by the international community since then. A big step was made in 1997 by the agreement of the Kyoto Protocol which was enforced in 2005. The UN climate change conference held in 2007 reached new commitments on the post-Kyoto Protocol agenda. The "Bali roadmap" is a positive step towards defining the next global regime to combat climate change. It should lead to a new agreement that will help to move beyond provisions of the Kyoto Protocol which ends in 2012. Thus, UN's leadership through UNFCC should be respected. Other organizations, like EU, G8, APEC and EAS have also made efforts in meeting the challenges of climate change.

As climate change is a common challenge of the international community, it calls for the widest possible international cooperation. However, developed countries, due to their long historical and current high per capita emission records, should take the lead to reduce GHG emissions, while other countries should contribute to addressing climate change in accordance with their responsibilities and capabilities. As estimated, under the best case scenarios of international action to keep greenhouse gas concentrations low, the need for adaptation measures will cost developing countries $10 billion annually just for infrastructure adjustments to floods, storm surges, water shortages, cyclones and other increased risks. Most of these relate to changes in hydrological conditions. Furthermore, "climate proofing" of project investments has to be done because this will affect the underlying assumptions behind the design of hydropower, water supply, irrigation, flood protection and even sanitation projects.[8]

Thus managing climate change must be coordinated with economic development. It is very important to make full use of the potential of advanced technology to address climate change. Developing countries do not have advanced technologies and international technology cooperation is urgently needed. For example, GHG emissions reduction needs the de-carbonizing of economic development through energy efficiency, development of renewable energy, nuclear energy, carbon capture and storage, etc. Therefore, technology plays a critical role in addressing climate change and international cooperation on technology R&D, deployment and transfer is of great importance. It is necessary that a technology cooperation mechanism be set up to enable developing countries to have access to advanced technologies. In this regard, assistance from developed countries in financial resources and capacity-building needs to be resolved along with technology cooperation.

Due to poor infrastructure, low level of development and fragile eco-systems, developing countries are vulnerable to the adverse effects of climate change, such as floods, droughts, tornados, etc. In the past, too much emphasis was put on mitigation. Adaptation must be put on an equal footing with mitigation and be integrated in future measures to address climate change.

III. Environment and Energy Cooperation in East Asia

East Asia has developed several cooperative mechanisms for the environment and energy.

---

[8] Haruhiko Kuroda (2008). Challenges for the Asian Economy in 2008 and Beyond. Speech at ADBI.

In Northeast Asia, China, Japan and Republic of Korea (ROK) have established cooperation by institutionalizing the tripartite ministerial meeting. For example, the eighth Tripartite Environment Ministers Meeting (TEMM) in 2006 declared that the three countries would "take various measures to build an environment-friendly and resource-saving society respectively".[9] Six countries — China, Japan, ROK, Russia, Mongolia and PDRK, since 1993 also have a cooperation mechanism in this area. At the 12th SOM meeting in 2007 an initiative on eco efficiency partnership was made.

In Southeast Asia, ASEAN has launched several projects on the environment and energy saving, and developed ASEAN+ frameworks with China, Japan, ROK, India, Australia on environment protection and energy cooperation. During the 11th ASEAN–China Summit in Singapore on 20 November 2007, the two sides decided to formulate an ASEAN–China Environmental Protection Cooperation Strategy. ASEAN and ROK launched their project on restoration of the degraded forest ecosystem in the Southeast Asian Region.

In East Asia, ASEAN+3 have agreed on regional coordination for integrated protection and management of the coastal and marine environments. The energy cooperation also covers energy security, cross-border energy trade and investment in the development of energy interconnection networks in the region. At the fourth meeting of the 10+3 energy cooperation ministers on 23 August 2007, the ministers proposed to increase energy efficiency which is considered as the best way to enhance energy security and solve climate change. Under the Greater Mekong Sub-region (GMS) environmental cooperation mechanism, the environment ministers spelled out the bio-diversity conservation corridor program for the sub-region and other cooperative projects.

EAS has played an active role in promoting environment and energy cooperation. At the second EAS, the leaders signed the

---

[9] Joint Communique of The Eighth Tripartite Environment Ministers Meeting among China, Japan and Korea, 2–3 December 2006.

Cebu Declaration on East Asian Energy Security and agreed to explore various areas of cooperation and projects by establishing an Energy Cooperation Task Force and convening an EAS Energy Ministers Meeting. At the third EAS, leaders signed the Singapore Declaration on Climate Change, Energy and the Environment and determined to intensify ongoing cooperation to improve energy efficiency, and the use of cleaner energy, including the use of renewable and alternative sources.[10]

Countries in East Asia have increasingly recognized the need for regional as well as international co-operation on environmental matters and have set out to create a variety of organizations, action plans, agreements, talks, and networks for co-operation. However, overall regional environmental cooperation in East Asia has been more discussed than acted on. Although there are serious environmental problems that require a certain level of regional co-operation, such as acid rain, marine resource protection and yellow dust, the countries have to this point failed to deploy and implement concrete action plans to tackle these problems.

ADB's active role should be encouraged since it will continue to play an important role in initiating and supporting the environment and energy cooperation. For example, ADB has initiated the Clean Energy and Environment Program, the Energy Efficiency Initiative, Carbon Market Initiative, Sustainable Clean Air Initiative for Asian Cities and Transport Initiative etc., and also helped to develop knowledge hubs by establishing research institutes on environment and energy technologies in India, China and Thailand.

Public awareness and participation is crucial for meeting the challenges of climate change. Fortunately, NGOs in East Asia have become increasingly active in addressing and acting on the problems of climate change. The cooperation between civil society and government has been developed.

---

[10] See Cebu Declaration on East Asian Energy Security 2006; Singapore Declaration on Climate Change, Energy and the Environment 2007.

IV. Environment and Energy Cooperation under EAS

EAS has become an important vehicle in initiating and promoting environment and energy cooperation in East Asia. Both at the Cebu and Singapore EAS meetings, leaders have drafted the blueprint of environment and energy cooperation. The participating countries determined to take concrete actions to improve energy efficiency and the use of cleaner energy, including the use of renewable and alternative sources. Considering that most of EAS members are developing economies, it is important to mobilize the financial support and cooperation for capacity-building. As stated in the Singapore Declaration, actions would be taken to encourage the deployment of clean technology in the region through various means, such as investment, technical and financial assistance, technology transfer, exchanging of scientific and technical expertise in partnership with international experts, and enhancing cooperation towards joint research and development of appropriate adaptation measures, supporting the development and expansion of policy and measures, including innovative instruments and financing mechanisms for environmental management, to promote sustainable patterns of consumption and production, as well as promoting public awareness of the impacts.[11]

CEPEA can serve as a valuable framework in designing and implementing environment and energy cooperation in East Asia. As an immediate arrangement, EAS can put on CEPEA's agenda the implementing of the Cebu and Singapore declarations. This may take dual approaches: individual and collective action plans. For the individual action plan, member countries should set goals and concrete action plans for improving energy efficiency and reduction of GHG. For the collective action plan, the cooperation should include:

— An East Asia regional goal of an environment-friendly and energy-saving economy, and in this connection, liberalization

---

[11] See Cebu Declaration on East Asian Energy Security 2006; Singapore Declaration on Climate Change, Energy and the Environment 2007.

of barriers affecting environmental goods and services should be considered.
— Work plan for cooperation on clean energy focusing on promoting energy efficiency, biomass and utilization of clean coal.
— Setting up an East Asian Foundation for environment and energy cooperation.

EAS environment and energy cooperation should complement other existing regional mechanisms such as the ASEAN, ASEAN+1s, ASEAN+3, APEC, ADB, World Bank and other regional as well as international organizations.

CHAPTER TWELVE

China's Economic Emergence and Regional Cooperation[1]

Introduction

The continuous high growth of China's economy and its growing impact on the rest of the world, especially the neighboring region, has received increasing attention. In 2003, China's GDP rate was as high as 9.1 percent and its foreign trade exceeded US$850 billion. Optimistic watchers argued that, considering its immense potential, China's high economic growth trend will continue for another decade or two. It is estimated that, within a few years, China's economy will be the third largest in the world after the United States and Japan, and may be the second largest after the US within two or three decades.

China's economic power has generated important both challenges and opportunities for the rest of the world. Its contribution to the world economy, and to the regional economy in particular, has grown larger. For some years, China's economic growth is one of the key factors behind world economic growth. At the same time, its economic growth has generated bigger domestic demand; thus, China's capacity for imports has been greatly enhanced.

---

[1] Paper was written for the conference held by KIEP, South Korea on East Asian Economic relations in March of 2004.

China's economic emergence is based highly on its "opening up" policy. China has a very high trade-GDP ratio and the largest market for FDI flow among developing economies. As a result, the Chinese economy has been increasingly integrated into the world economy, and to the Asia-Pacific region in particular. FDI plays a significant role in supporting China's economic growth. A striking feature of FDI is that they are not just a single direction flow. FDIs in China are closely interconnected to those in other countries. Following China's economic emergence, a new network of production and services has been developed based on the linkages of FDIs, which has been witnessed especially in the Asia-Pacific region. The intra-regional economic activities are increasingly based on exchange of parts, components and other intermediate products, reflecting the development of intricate intra-regional production networks, in which production processes are sub-divided among many different countries.[2]

The new economic convergence in the Asia-pacific region, and in the East Asian region in particular, has created greater interest for the economies in the region to strengthen their economic cooperation and integration. Regional trade arrangements (RTAs) are considered to be rational on at least the following factors: one is to realize harmonization through institutional arrangements (rules, standards, regulations, policies); another is to work through collective management of crisis-prevention (contagion). China's economic emergence has become a stimulating new factor to facilitate RTAs. Due to its closer economic integration to the region, China has become more and more interested in RTAs after its accession to WTO.

The East Asian region used to be one of the few regions without RTAs. This is changing. ASEAN started its own AFTA as early as in 1992, but real progress (if taking intra-regional trade as an indicator) was slow for quite some time. The 1997 financial crisis gave a great push to regional cooperation which gave birth to the "10 plus 3" (TPT) process. TPT is still a regional dialogue forum for

---

[2] The World Bank (2003). *East Asia Update: Looking Beyond Short-term Shocks*, p. 15.

East Asia. But seems to be it leading to a more institutionalized East Asian regionalism in the direction of an East Asian FTA (EAFTA) and an East Asian community as recommended by the East Asian Vision Group (EAVG). Its future may be too early to predict, but the direction seems clear. China has shown its great interest and is playing an active role. China's active participation in the East Asian cooperation process is due to its successful economic development.

I. China's Economic Growth Trend

China has achieved remarkable progress in economic development since its reform and opening-up policy. Statistics show that the average growth rate of Chinese GDP is as high as 9.4 percent from 1979–2002. In the first half of the 1990s, the Chinese economy experienced over-heating with its growth rate hitting even 12 percent; with a successful readjustment policy, it came down to 7.6 percent during the second half.[3] The growth rates slowed down to about 7 percent after 1997 with the negative effect of the Asian financial crisis though China avoided a direct crisis. Growth has started to move up again since 2000, to 9.1 percent in 2003, an unexpected high rate even with the impact of SARS in the first half of the year. It is truly exceptional for China to keep to such high economic growth for so long. Today, China is the world's fifth largest economy in GDP terms and has moved up the ranks to a middle-income country according to GDP/per capita level (exceeding US$1000 in 2003).

A sizeable middle class has emerged. Thus, the internal strength supporting Chinese economic growth will be gradually built up. In new sectors, like telecommunications, the number of mobile phone, internet and computer users in China is among the world's highest. It is expected that domestic consumption, other

---

[3] World Bank (2003). *China Country Economic Memorandum: Promoting Growth with Equity*. Washington DC, p. 15.

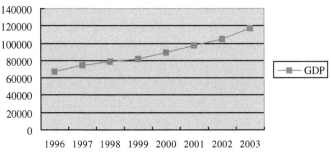

Source: China Statistical Yearbook, www.cei.gov.cn

Figure 1: Growth trend of China's GDP (in 100 mil. RMB, 1US Dollar = 8.27 RMB).

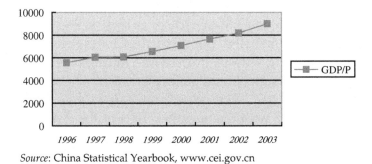

Source: China Statistical Yearbook, www.cei.gov.cn

Figure 2: Growth trend of China's GDP/Per Capita (in RMB, 1US Dollar = 8.27 RMB).

than exports, may become the major strength to sustain future economic growth.

At the same time, China's production capacity has significantly increased, and it has become among the world's largest or the largest producer of color TV sets, refrigerators, DVD players, computers etc. China's exports have increased remarkably to ask as the world's fourth largest. If the current trend continues, China may become the world's second largest country in terms of foreign trade by 2005, and in terms of GDP by 2025 after the United States.

Due to its huge population size — one-fifth of the world's population, together with its successful economic development,

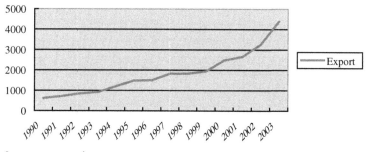

Source: www.mofcom.gov.cn

Figure 3: China's export growth (1990–2003) (in US$100 million).

China owns great potential in expanding its market. Thus, China has become increasingly attractive to foreign investors. Until 2003, the accumulated FDI in China exceeded US$500 billion. Except for a few years of slow-down after the 1997 financial crisis, FDI flow to China has increased continuously since the 1990s in both annual growth rate and volume. The FDI enterprises have played a special role in making the Chinese economy dynamic since they have not only contributed more than half of the exports, but also invested intensively in new industries.

Chinese economic growth is highly dependent on outside factors. Among them, import and export trade capital inflow and the global economic situation are the most important. Export/GDP ratio has been on an increasingly high level, which means that there is a close correlation between the expansion of exports and growth of China's GDP. The contribution of exports to Chinese economic growth has become much larger in recent years. However, from a long-term perspective, such a pattern of growth is not sustainable. No large economy in the world has so high an export/GDP ratio. Considering the gradual built-up of domestic consumption and increasing accumulated FDI production capacity in China, the export expansion will have to continue in the years to come.

The majority of economists in China seem optimistic about China's longer-term economic development. They argued that

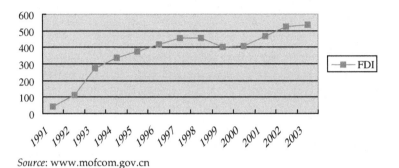

Source: www.mofcom.gov.cn

Figure 4: Annual FDI inflow to China (1991–2003) (in US$100 million).

China has entered a new period for economic restructuring and growth.[4] The high growth trend may last for another 20 years. Nevertheless, such long-term high economic growth may create serious imbalance.

Chinese economic growth still largely follows the traditional industrialization model with high raw material and energy consumption. Due to its low efficiency, the input/output ratio of production in China is only one third to one fifth of many developed economies. The result: high economic growth rate creates unreasonable demand for raw materials and energy. In 2003, China's oil consumption surpassed Japan and become the second largest only after the United States. China's steel consumption accounts for more than one third of total world steel consumption. China's increasing demand for imports have significantly affected its own economy and the world market.

The Chinese economy is under restructuring and in transition. Many difficulties and destabilizing factors will continue to exist. Among them, a high ratio of bad bank loans, restructuring of state-owned enterprises and a huge surplus of rural labor will have great impact on future economic sustainability and social stability. Many scholars have warned that while the world enjoys the benefits brought by China's continuous high economic

---

[4] Xiao Bin (2003). Chinese economic expansion can be sustainable. www.chinanews. com.cn/407111.html/2003

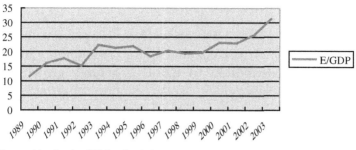

Source: Yearbook of China Statistics.

Figure 5: Ratio of export to GDP in Chinese economy.

growth, China has to prepare for the possible risk of a sudden slowdown, or even a crisis in the economy.[5] Nevertheless, there is no immediate risk of a slowdown since its growth potential has not been fully realized as a large developing and transitional economy. The Chinese government has a high capacity to manage the macroeconomic stability.

II. Impacts of Chinese Economic Growth

China's economic emergence has greatly impacted the world economy. For some years, given its high economic growth, quick expansion of exports and continuous large inflow of FDI, and the WTO accession, China was described as "a threat" because of worries that China would take away market share and investments from others. But with China's growing role in creating large imports and stimulating the regional economies, China has also been seen as a positive factor.[6] However, the debates on China's economic emergence will continue because of both stable and unstable factors.

---

[5] The "worst scenario" for the Chinese economy has been always raised since so many problems exist. Pamela C.M. Mar & Frank-Jurgen Richter (2003). *China: Enabling a New Era of Changes*. World Economic Forum, p. 7.

[6] As pointed out by Mr. Stanley Fischer, "There is little cause for fear, a big dynamic economy in the neighborhood is a benefit," "Don't fear China threat" (4 September 2001). *The Straits Times*.

1. *Growth contribution and challenge*

China's share of global GDP grew from 1.7 percent in 1990 to 3.9 percent in 2002. It is clear that China's economic growth has made a great contribution to world economic growth. China contributed one quarter of world economic growth during 1995–2002. In the past 4 years, China and the United States contributed two-thirds of the new output of the world economy.[7] Although China's economic weight is still limited, its role as an added value (a large increment) in stabilizing and stimulating the world economy, and the regional economy in particular, has been greatly enhanced.

China's economic growth is based on an open model. However, the outside linkage of the Chinese economy is significantly weighted in the Asia-Pacific region, and in the East Asian region in particular. Two-thirds of China's foreign trade and almost 90 percent of FDI inflow come from the Asia–Pacific region, and more than half of the foreign trade and 70 percent of FDI inflow from East Asia. The greatest impact of the Chinese economic surge has been witnessed in the Asia-Pacific region and to East Asia in particular. As the Chinese economy becomes bigger (its size is larger than the total of all East Asian economies excluding Japan), its high growth significantly shapes the curves of the regional economies.

Since Japan, as the largest economy in the region, has been experiencing a decade-long slow growth, China's economic emergence has played a special role in supporting regional economic stability. Japanese imports from and FDI to the East Asian region have declined after the financial crisis in 1997. The regional economy would be much worse if not for China's high economic growth. We have witnessed a positive linear relationship between Chinese economic growth and the rest of the economies in East Asia in recent years.

---

[7] JETRO (2003). White paper on international trade and foreign direct investment, summary, p. 4; 2 December 2003, *Asian Wall Street Journal*, p. 1; Business Week, 2 February 2004, p. 12.

At the same time, China's high growth has also created challenges. China's high economic growth has relied highly on the expansion of exports and large inflow of FDI. Has China taken away market share from others and dried up the FDI flow? China faces competition from its East Asian neighbours for the world's market. According to C.H. Kwan, the competition between China and East Asian economies on the US market increased remarkably during the 1990s; the competition ratios between China and Indonesia were as high as 82.8 percent, Thailand 65.4 percent, Malaysia 48.7 percent, The Philippines 46.1 percent, S. Korea 37.5 percent, and Japan 16.3 percent in terms of value in 2000.[8] However, one should be careful with the figures on "product similarity" since each country may be significantly different in each product category and level as well as quality of the product. Although the trade-offs between China's exports and the exports of the other East Asian developing economies are not clear,[9] it does not mean that there is no trade-off for specific products. As a matter of fact, China is also facing competition from other developing economies in low cost products and the discriminated arrangement of quotas in textile exports.

China has been criticized for taking away capital resources from others since it has continuously received the lion's share of FDI to developing economies. FDI's critical role in sustaining China's high economic growth is seen in its attraction for investments by MNCs which are drawn to China's improving economic condition and potential domestic market in particular. ASEAN is often seen as a looser in competing with China for FDI flows. This is misleading since the slowdown of FDI to ASEAN after the 1997 financial crisis is not because of China's competition, but because of the region's worsened economic and political situation. China

---

[8] C. H. Kwan (2002). Overcoming Japan's "China Syndrome". Paper presented the *Conference Asian Economic Integration*, RIETI, p. 8.
[9] Kathic Krumm and Homi Kharas (2003). East Asia Integrates — A trade policy agenda for shared growth. World Bank, p. 12

enjoys some special advantages in attracting more FDI flow: abundant labor supply, low costs and a huge potential market in its large population. The resources that can be used for FDI are diverse and not fixed. Thus, to a large extent, FDI flow to China is not a trade-off for FDI to other economies. In fact, we have already seen the recovery of FDI flow to some ASEAN countries in recent years due to their improved economic situation.[10] In the long-term, it is vulnerable for an economy to be too dependent on FDI flow. The Chinese economy would become less dynamic if it does not progress in its own innovation capacity.

2. *Network building*

FDI flow to China is not a side story since investments in China have close connections to those in other economies linked by the networks of the multinational companies (MNCs). Based on its large accumulated investments and production capacity, China has become a production hub in developing network linkages not just between the host and the home countries, but also with many other economies. This kind of network is considered to be a kind of "parallel development", different from the traditional vertical and hierarchic transfer of technology.[11] That is to say, with its continuous high economic growth, China is increasingly "a central player" in this production network, which seems beneficial significantly to regional economic growth.[12] David Roland-Holst called this a phenomenon of "bamboo capitalism" in East Asia since this culminating feature of the FDI-driven supply chain has created diverse and vibrant local industries around the East Asian region. The further the supply chains (the root system) are decomposed

---

[10] The Japanese accumulated FDI volume in ASEAN is still four times that of China today.

[11] It is called as "a new paradigm for East Asian economic development". Chen Yu-shi (2002). A new paradigm shift in East Asian economic studies. *Ritsumeikan Journal of Asia Pacific Studies*, 10, p. 10.

[12] Kathic Krumm and Homi Kharas (2003). p. 23.

and extended geographically, the faster and more profuse will be the proliferation of new enterprises.[13] This new development in East Asia signifies that this region may accumulate new strength for future economic dynamism.

3. Import surge

With its very high ratio of foreign trade/GDP, China's high growth generates sizable trade exchanges. The direct impact of Chinese economic growth to the region is its import surge. China became the third largest import market after the US and Germany in 2003. China's import in 2003 is close to eight times that of 1990, almost doubled that of 2000–2003. This trend seems to be strengthening. The increase of China's imports greatly helps the exports of many economies. China's increasing demand, especially for raw materials, also helps to raise the export price level, a positive contribution to resource-exporting economies.

The importance of China as a big import market is well demonstrated by comparing the trend of exports to two the largest economies, the United States and Japan. The exports of ASEAN as

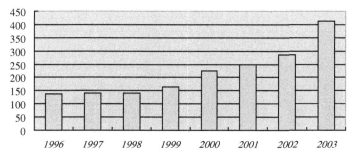

Source: Yearbook of China statistics, www.mofcom.gov.cn

Figure 6:   China's import growth.

---

[13] David Roland-Holst, Iwan Aziz and Li Gang Liu (2003). Regionalism and globalism: East and Southeast Asian trade relations in wake of China's WTO accession. ADB Institute Research Paper Series, XX, p. 16.

a whole to China has quadrupled in the past two decades, raising its share of China's imports close to 10 percent. The share of NIE's (Singapore, S. Korea, Hong Kong and Taiwan) exports to China has now surpassed their share to the United States. All East Asian economies increased their export share on the Chinese market. The exports share to China from East Asian economies rose from 8 percent in 1990 to 16 percent in 2002, higher than to Japan, and close to the US.[14] The strength of China's imports comes from two sources: one is the increase of its own demand due to the expansion of domestic consumption; another is the surge of exports, i.e. imports for exports. Looking ahead, the increase of internal demand in China will be more significant with rising levels of domestic income since there is a positive linkage between import increase and per unit of GDP in China.

The figures for 2003 typically shows the influence of China as a big market for regional exports. China's total foreign trade increased 25 percent, to US$851.2 billion; imports increased 40 percent, to US$413 billion, US$126 billion more than 2002. China's imports from ASEAN and S. Korea increased more than 50 percent; from Japan, close to 40 percent; from the US, close to

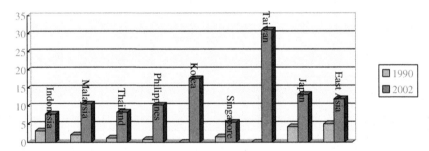

Note: The share represents the export percentage to China of total exports. Figure for Indonesia, Malaysia, Philippines are for 2001.
Source: www.mofcom.gov.cn; www.aseansec.org

Figure 7:   Export share to China.

---

[14] The World Bank (2003). *East Asia Update*, p. 15.

25 percent.[15] For many economies, exports to China represent the lion's share in their trade increase: for Japan, 70 percent of its export increase in 2003 is to China; for S. Korea, 40 percent; even for the United States, 25 percent. For many Japanese products, the Chinese market is the major export destination. According to Japanese trade statistics Japan–China trade value exceeded Japan–US trade value in 2003 for the first time. Export surge to China has become an important factor to stimulate Japanese economic recovery in 2003.[16]

China's market still has big potential. By 2003 China is already Asia's largest individual importer. If this trend continues, by 2020 China's foreign trade size may equal the U.S. With its growing integration with the East Asian region, China will play a unique role in recycling capital through its trade balance in the East Asian region. According to Holst, Aziz and Liu, in the next two decades, China will gain a huge trade surplus with US and EU, while at the same time, a large trade deficit with East Asia.[17] More than that, it is expected that China may become another important engine for world economic growth (and the regional economies in particular) based on its sizable increase of domestic consumption parallel to the United States.

Currently the surge of China's imports is still highly reliant on its export expansion since about half of China's imports are for exports, with an even much higher proportion of imports in the area of manufactured parts. A domestic consumption-led import structure still needs to be built up.

On the other hand, China's huge import increase has inflated prices sharply for many goods, especially for some raw materials and energy. This is a double-edge sword which also raises the cost of economic activities.[18]

---

[15] Economic Daily, 27 February 2004, p. 2.

[16] Economic Daily, 3 December 2003; Lianhe Zaobao, 17 February 2004.

[17] David Roland-Holst, Iwan Aziz and Li Gang Liu (2003). p. 19.

[18] We saw significant increase in prices of steel, oil and some other raw materials on the world market in 2003 due to China's import surge.

III. China and East Asian Regionalism

1. *Emerging regionalism*

The East Asian cooperation process started as an emergency response to the financial crisis. When the Asian financial crisis broke out within ASEAN in 1997, the whole East Asian region was plunged into great difficulty. This led to the first 'ASEAN plus three' (China, Japan and ROK) (APT) leaders' meeting in Kuala Lumpur in 1997. The aim of the meeting was to deal with the crisis through regional cooperation. This is an important historical event since it started the regional cooperation process with shared regional interests and a newly defined regional identity, i.e. East Asia.

East Asian cooperation has generated more and more governmental involvement and institution-building.[19] At the same time, regionalism in East Asia finds its rationale in not just economic benefits, but also political interests. Comparing with other regions, East Asia is late in forging RTA and other institutional establishments. Aside from intra-regional desire for a closer partnership, East Asian new regionalism is also considered to be a rational response to the progress of other regions.[20]

Until now, an integrated framework for East Asian cooperation is emerging. The major one is annual leaders' meeting for official dialogue and consultation on regional immediate and long-term issues ranging from economic situation, macro-economic policy, sub-regional development to political stability as well as security. Although the leaders' meeting is divided into several tracks, i.e. ASEAN 10, ASEAN to 1 (China, Japan and South Korea separately),

---

[19] Shujiro Urata argued "a shift from market-led to institutional-led regional economic integration in East Asia", paper prepared for the conference on Asian economic integration organized by Research Institute of Economy, Trade and Industry, Japan, April 22–23, 2002, Tokyo, p. 1.

[20] It is considered that Prime Minister Mahathir's proposal of forming East Asian Economic Caucus (EAEC) is a direct response to NAFTA. Peter Drysdale & Kenichi Ishigaki editors, East Asian trade and financial integration, New issues, Asia-Pacific Press, Canberra, 2002, p. 6.

3 (China, Japan and ROK) and ASEAN plus 3, they are all under a regional framework. Aside from leaders' meeting, there are many tracks of ministers' meetings.

East Asian cooperation process has moved beyond simple dialogue. Some real institutional arrangements have been developed. Among them, Chang Mai Initiative (CMI), i.e. swap arrangements among East Asian countries, is the most significant, which may leads further to a higher level financial and monetary integration for East Asia. East Asian FTA (EAFTA) has not been on the agenda yet, but different efforts are made in moving toward this direction.

However, the major concern is still there: what is the direction of this process? EAVG recommended an "East Asian Free Trade Area (EAFTA)", "the East Asian summit", gradual monetary integration, regional institutional building and finally, toward a regional entity — "East Asia community (EAC)".[21] This is the first time for East Asia to have a clearly dressed long-term vision by eminent persons. However, it is not easy to reach consensus on these recommendations among all partners.

Considering great diversity of East Asian region and complexity of the relations among the countries, the process of East Asian cooperation and integration can only follow a pragmatic approach. It is necessary to encourage multi-layered arrangements and gradually move to a unique regional framework.

Institutional building is inevitable for the process of East Asian cooperation. Although the institutional building starts from low level and on a multi-layered structure, progress will be made along with the development.

2. *Economic foundation*

The foundation of East Asian regionalism is its growing economic integration through intra-regional trade and investment. Intra-regional trade in East Asia started to accelerate from the late 1980s,

---

[21] East Asian Vision Group Report, 2001.

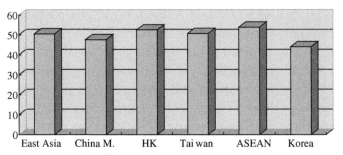

Source: JETRO, Perspective on East Asian FTA, March, 2003, p. 42.

Figure 8: Intra-regional trade in East Asia.

which reached as high a level as 50 percent of all trade from the region before the financial crisis. It began to decline after 1997 with the negative impact of the financial crisis, but climbed to 50.5 percent again in 2001. The ratio of intra-regional trade has continued to increase since. The intra-regional exports of East Asia's eight economies rose 13 percent, as compared to an increase of exports to the rest of world of only three percent in 2002. Exports of these economies to East Asia contributed two-thirds of their total export increase in the same year.[22] China's import surge has enhanced the trend of intra-regional trade in the East Asian region. This helps to change the views on China's economic emergence from being a threat to that of an opportunity.

Importantly, this intra-regional trade is increasingly based on exchange of parts, components and other intermediate products, reflecting the development of intricate intra-regional production networks, in which production processes are subdivided among many different countries.[23] FDI flow plays a key role in creating this network. In the future China will change from being a market receiving FDI inflow to become an important resource for FDI outflow. This kind of network based on exchange of trade and

---

[22] The eight economies are: Indonesia, Korea, Malaysia, Philippines, Singapore, Taiwan (China), Thailand and Vietnam.
[23] The World Bank (2003). *East Asia Update: Looking Beyond Short Term Shocks*, p. 15.

capital has profound impact on East Asian economic development and interest for cooperation and integration.

3. *China' active role*

China has become active in joining the regional trade arrangement after its accession of WTO. A surprising move is its initiative to forge a FTA with ASEAN. This shows its new interest and confidence in regionalism.

In 2000 in Singapore, having achieved WTO accession, Chinese Premier Zhu Rongji proposed a free trade arrangement with ASEAN. The following year, leaders of China and ASEAN agreed to establish a free trade area (FTA) within 10 years, and the framework agreement was signed in late 2002.

The question has often been raised: Why did China make such an initiative? The answer lies in its growing confidence and the potential gains. The establishment of a FTA between China and ASEAN will create an economic region with huge benefits.[24] ASEAN would gain from easy market access to China and improving its own investment environment. The significance of establishing a FTA between China and ASEAN goes beyond economic benefits. The close economic integration will contribute immensely to peace and stability between China and ASEAN, and the East Asian region. China–ASEAN FTA will press Japan and also ROK to formulate trade arrangements with ASEAN.

In fact, China plays a key role in driving East Asia toward a new regionalism. China believes that East Asian regional cooperation and integration could help to create a stable and cooperative environment, which is crucial for realizing its ambitious modernization.

---

[24] According to the simulation conducted by the ASEAN Secretariat, a China–ASEAN FTA will increase ASEAN's export to China by 48 percent and China's export to ASEAN by 55.1 percent. It will increase China's GDP by 0.3 percent or by US$2.2 billion in absolute terms; ASEAN's GDP by 0.9 percent or by US$5.4 billion. See "Forging closer ASEAN–China economic relations in the twenty-first century", report by ASEAN–China Expert Group on Economic Cooperation, 2001.

China's active role in promoting East Asian regional integration has been accepted by its regional partners.

China has great development potential. Due to its size, the impact of China's economic emergence is significant and comprehensive, be it its high growth, or a slowdown. Never has a country with such a huge population changed so quickly in such a short time. This is a challenge both to China and the rest of the world.

We have witnessed a changing China, not just in economic power, but also in other areas. However, what China requires is not order for domination and control, but for development in a peaceful and favorable environment. This may help us to understand why China should identify its development as a "peaceful rise". Such a strategy has been reflected in China's recent active responses in its foreign policy.

CHAPTER THIRTEEN

China's Accession to WTO and Its Impact on China–ASEAN Relations[1]

Geographically, China and ASEAN are closely linked. Economically, they are complementary. The two will benefit significantly if they form a close economic partnership based on legal arrangements for liberalization, facilitation and cooperation in the areas of trade, investment and services. ASEAN is anxious about China's accession to WTO since China will become more competitive in expanding exports and attracting foreign direct investment (FDI). Actually, a more open and dynamic Chinese economy will provide great opportunities for ASEAN. The benefits will be even larger if the two could formulate a vast economic area through the development of the FTA.

I. China's WTO commitments

After 15 years of hard negotiations China's[2] membership of WTO has been settled. China has already made great progress during this long process of evolution. The annual average GDP

---

[1] This is a revised version of the report written for China–ASEAN Official Expert Group report on feasibility study of FTA in 2001. Thanks to Dr. Zhao Jianglin and Zhou Xiaobin for their contribution.

[2] Herein China is referred to as mainland China.

growth of the Chinese economy was 9.3 percent from 1986 to 2000, now the seventh largest economy in the world. China is increasingly on the list of the world's leading producers in many areas, for example, it is now the largest producer of steel, coal, chemical fertilizer, meat, cotton etc. With the increasing income levels of its people, national consumption is constantly shooting up. With the largest population in the world, China has the best market potential.

It has emerged as a major trading economy. Its foreign trade has expanded from US$100 billion to US$474.3 billion during 1986 to 2000. It is now the world's seventh largest in merchandized foreign trade, the seventh largest exporter, and eighth largest importer. The strengths supporting this significant progress are its reform and "opening" policies. The Chinese economy has become more and more liberalized and integrated with the world market. Trade tariff barriers have been largely reduced; total tariff rates fell from 42 percent to 15.3 percent as a whole from 1990 to 2000 with remarkable reduction of non-tariff measures (NTM) at the same time, with currently only less than 200 import items under license control. The Chinese economy has benefited significantly from liberalization given the clear linkage between openness and economic growth.[3]

With the opening-up of the Chinese economy, and its advantages of cheap labor and great market potential, FDI[4] has increased noticeably into China. From 1986–2000, actual or utilized FDI in China increased at an average annual rate of more than 20 percent, with a cumulative total of US$339 billion in 2000. China has become the largest recipient of FDI in the Asian region, the second largest in the world after the US. FDI plays a very important role in the Chinese economy. The dynamic growth of foreign invested enterprises (FIEs) is an important factor supporting Chinese economic dynamism. The role of FIEs in China's foreign trade is

---

[3] Peter Drysdale and Ligang Song (ed.) (2000). *China's entry into WTO: strategic issues and quantitative assessments*, London and New York: Routledge.
[4] FDI includes that from Hong Kong, Macao and Taiwan.

even more significant. FIEs' contributions to China's exports and imports are 47.9 percent and 51 percent respectively in 2000, more than double that of the early 1990s. FIEs do not just bring in capital; more importantly, they bring management and technology. As a matter of fact, FIEs, both as investors and competitors, have helped to change Chinese economic structures and pushing local enterprises, especially state-owned enterprises (SOEs), to change themselves.

In its negotiations for entry into WTO, China has committed to a very comprehensive package of market liberalization to be implemented immediately after its entry into WTO. China is given about five years to fulfill its commitments whose major points are:

— The general tariff level for all industrial goods will be down to 10 percent within five years from the current 15 percent. China agrees to bind all of its tariffs, i.e. not to raise its tariff level.
— Almost all administrative examination and approval procedures on imported goods, i.e. quotas, licenses and other non-tariff quantitative restrictions will be abolished within five years. Trading rights for foreign companies will be granted.
— A broad range of professional services, like wholesale and retail trade, as well as after-sales service, repair, maintenance and transportation will be liberalized, with foreign ownership allowed up to 49 percent.
— By participating in the WTO Information Technology Agreement (ITA), all tariffs on IT equipment, computers, computer equipment and other IT products will be eliminated, i.e. zero tariff rate by 2003.
— With acceptation of the principles of WTO Agreement on Basic Telecommunications, China will allow the provision of any basic telecommunication service, including local, long distance and international service by any means of technology within two to six years, allowing 49 percent foreign investment in all services and 50 percent foreign ownership for value-added and paging services.
— Financial services will be liberalized, thus opening the market to banking, insurance, securities, fund management and other

financial service. Licenses will be awarded solely on the basis of prudential criteria, with no economic-needs test or quantitative limits on the number of licenses issued. All geographical restrictions on where foreign banks can offer domestic currency services will be lifted with no numerical limits on number of foreign banks and insurance companies that will be licensed as of 2005.

— The average statutory tariff rate of agriculture products will be reduced from 22 percent to 14.5 percent. A tariff-rate quota system for key products, such as wheat, corn, rice, soybean oil, cotton etc, will be established and all non-tariff barriers to imports will be replaced by tariff rate-based measures. Agricultural subsidies will be reduced, with the commitment of "yellow box" subsidy not exceeding 8.5 percent of total value of agricultural products.

China has agreed to comprehensive liberalization commitments in the WTO negotiations with ASEAN countries. According to the agreements, the average basic tariff level for ASEAN products will be reduced by 34 percent to 47 percent within five years which is faster than the general reduction. Thus, trade barriers between China and ASEAN countries will be largely reduced.

The entry into WTO represents a new stage of China's economic reform and "opening-up" to the outside world, i.e. from a kind of selective liberalization to comprehensive liberalization, from experimental liberalization to legal and accountable liberalization, from unilateral liberalization to WTO rule-based liberalization. It will integrate China's economy with the international system.

Liberalization, or open competition in the economy will enhance Chinese economic efficiency and promote industrial progress. Competition will force Chinese enterprises to improve technology and management, which will significantly benefit the Chinese economy in transferring it from quantitative to qualitative growth.

WTO is a rule-based international organization. As a WTO member, China will strictly adhere to all of its rules and accommodate its domestic rules and regulations with those of the WTO. This is considered to be one of the most important changes to the Chinese legal system as well as other systems. China's policy and regulations will become more transparent and accountable, which will provide a fair business environment for foreign partners in the Chinese market.

WTO accession will provide benefits to China in terms of the security of its access to world markets since Chinese products will benefit from WTO MFN system, for equal rights to enter other markets. At the same time, market access and trade disputes will be settled by WTO rules, this means Chinese companies need not face unfair treatment and discrimination in other market.

Some have argued that by fast liberalizing of the market, including sensitive and infant sectors, Chinese companies will meet stronger competition from foreign competitors. It is expected that Chinese imports will increase much faster which will reduce the large trade surplus, or even turn it to a trade deficit, especially in the first several years after joining WTO. Lots of enterprises in the less competitive sectors, like chemicals, medicine, automobile and agriculture may be forced to close down, thus increasing unemployment. Banking, insurance, as well as telecommunications which used to be highly protected may find themselves in a very disadvantageous situation in having to compete with foreign competitors. Considering the residual problems from the old planned economy and transformation into the market economy, the banking and insurance sectors may need more time to adjust and change. It is worrying that China's financial market may become very vulnerable to strong competition from foreign banks and insurance companies. China is also facing increasing regional disparity and income gaps among different groups of its population, which is considered one of the most serious social problems in its developing and transforming process. Fast liberalization and open competition brought by WTO commitments may make these problems worse.

However, from its experience of successful reform and "opening-up" to the outside world, China has the capacity to meet the challenges and manage its economic and social transformation well. As a matter of fact, the long process of the negotiations for WTO membership has given China the experience to prepare for change.

II. Effects on Chinese Economy

According to a World Bank study, China's WTO accession will have very positive welfare gain. The most significant impact is on its foreign trade, with an apparent increase of its share in world export by two percentage points higher than without accession.[5] A study by the Development Research Center (DRC) based on the CGE model, and using only estimates of tariff reduction, showed that WTO entry would boost China's average annual growth rate by a full percentage point, and exports and imports, 24 and 18 percent respectively. A study by the U.S. International Trade Commission (ITC) predicted a four percent increase in China's gross domestic product and 12 percent of exports, 14 percent imports.[6] However, there are some limits to these studies. Assumptions were based on conditions that existed in the mid-1990s which did not take into account the substantial economic restructuring in China in the years immediately prior to its entry into the WTO. In addition, they did not analyze all effects of China's accession to WTO, including trade facilitation such as intellectual property, government purchase, competition policy and so on, but only partial effects produced by trade liberalization such as tariff reduction and abolishing of non-tariff barriers as a result of WTO membership.

The pattern of Chinese economic growth adopted by the government is different from many of East–Asian countries, such as Japan and Republic of Korea (ROK). China has adopted a "pro-FDI" policy, and thus, both export-led production and

[5] Elana Lanchovichina and Will Martin (2001). Trade liberalization in China's accession to WTO, World Bank paper.

[6] Li Shangtong and Zhai Fan (2000). *Impact of WTO Accession on China's Economy – A Dynamic General Equilibrium Analysis*, Beijing, China.

domestic consumption potential developed very fast. It is clear that this FDI-led production becomes a very important force to strengthen domestic competition. Due to the increasing share of domestic sale of FDI products, the Chinese market has become increasingly competitive. WTO entry will make Chinese economy more efficient through real integration and standardization of management and regulations on an international level, especially for domestic enterprises.

The challenges to China are enormous, which may not come just from the change in trade environment, but also from domestic industrial updating. Although China has experienced rapid economic growth for over 20 years, the major source of economic growth has resulted from the rapid accumulation of production factors such as labor and capital and extraordinarily high rates of resource mobilization from low-efficient agriculture to high-efficient non-agriculture sectors. Improvement in total factor productivity associated with increasing efficiency in the use of scarce resources contributed to much less economic growth than in developed countries such as US and Japan, and, at the same time, led to a slow industrial transformation. WTO membership will probably result in a big social cost caused by readjustment in some sectors, but it also provides China with an opportunity to improve its technological advantage by accelerating domestic industrial restructuring and raise the level of Chinese participation in international production.

There have been great changes in the Chinese industrial sector since 1986 when China applied to GATT. The share of agriculture in GDP has decreased from 27.1 percent in 1986 to 17.7 percent in 1999 while the share of manufacturing and the share of services have increased from 44 percent and 28.9 percent in 1986 to 49.3 percent and 33 percent in 1999 respectively. At the same time, the share of labor-intensive goods in China's exports has decreased after it peaked in the mid-1990s, while the share of capital-intensive and technology-intensive goods in China's export began to rise after the mid-1990s. What has happened in the Chinese industrial sector was attributed to great readjustments, especially in 1990s.

The impacts of WTO accession on sectors are significant and various. Generally, due to the potential export surge, labor-intensive industries, such as garments and some capital-intensive sectors, such as chemicals, would benefit significantly. The large gains can be seen in apparel, footwear, metals, electronics, utilities and other light manufactures. According to the study, apparel export will benefit most, more than 1.5 times higher than without WTO accession.[7] But export of some labor-intensive products from China may loose the competitive edge since labor cost will fast increase. In addition, sub-regional agreements, such as NAFTA, provide internal favors for its members, which may improve restraints on China's exports to the region. On the other hand, FDI will probably shift direction from labor-intensive to capital-intensive and technology-intensive sectors or services. However, the effects on the capital-intensive and technology-intensive sectors may differ from one to the other, and real benefits will be highly reliant on their capability to meet the challenges.

WTO accession will help to enhance China's industrial technologies through a kind of "competitive improvement". Domestic companies will have to improve their technology in order to compete with foreign competition, while FDI will invest intensively in the capital-intensive and technology-intensive sectors in order to gain a larger share of China's market. Due to the elimination of restrictions on business activities, FDI will move to high potential sectors, like telecommunication, which will certainly force local companies to upgrade their technological and management skills quickly.

With the liberalization of the market, China's imports may increase faster, thus worsening its trade balance after joining WTO. The import surge may force many inefficient small and medium companies to close down. It is expected that imports of textiles, food grains, feed grains, beverage, metals, petrochemicals, as well as automobiles will increase remarkably.[8] The challenge to China's

---

[7] Elena Lanchovichina and Will Martin (2001).
[8] Elena Lanchovichina and Will Martin (2001).

agriculture sector comes from the pressure of cheaper imports and reduction of government subsidies, which may cause decline of rural income and rise of surplus labor. The challenge to China's services sector will be significant. Although China's service sector has gradually opened up, compared to the other sectors, the level of liberalization is lower. For example, the banking sector has to restructure itself quickly in order to meet the challenges.

III. Impact on China–ASEAN Trade Relations

Foreign trade is an important driving force for the economic development of China and ASEAN. In the 1990s, both China and ASEAN achieved high growth in foreign trade. During the decade from 1991 to 2000, China's foreign trade grew at an average annual rate of 15 percent. In 2000, China's exports amounted to US$249.2 billion and its imports totaled US$225.1 billion, and the ratio of its total foreign trade to its GDP stood at 44 percent. During the period from 1991 to 1996, ASEAN's foreign trade also grew at an average annual rate of 15 percent, but the rate was lowered during and after the financial crisis. However, ASEAN's ratio of foreign trade to GDP is much higher than that of China, for example, 134 percent in 1997, though it differs from one country to another, with very low levels for new ASEAN member economies.

ASEAN is one of China's most important trading partners. Its position in China's foreign merchandise trade has been continuously on the rise, with its proportion in China's total increasing from 5.8 percent in 1991 to 8.3 percent in 2000. It is now China's fifth biggest trading partner, next only to Japan, USA, European Union and Hong Kong. During the same period, ASEAN's proportion in China's total exports increased from 5.7 percent to 6.9 percent and ASEAN's proportion in China's total imports rose from six percent to 9.9 percent. In 2000, China's exports to ASEAN totaled US$17.3 billion and China's imports from ASEAN totaled US$22.2 billion, increasing respectively by 42.5 percent and 49.2 percent from the previous year.

China–ASEAN trade is characterized by an evident complementary nature, which affords an important basis for the two sides to further expand their bilateral trade. The commodities traded between China and ASEAN can be roughly divided into two categories. The first category are those with clear complementary character, which account for about half of the volume of their bilateral trade, and of which both parties have advantage over the other in respective products. The second category without a clear complementary nature also account for about half of their bilateral trade. Those in the first category are basically characterized by the differences in their material resources. The commodities which the ASEAN has advantage are: mineral products (including mineral fuels), plastics/rubber, wood and wood articles, pulp and paper, fats and oils. They account for 42 percent of China's imports from ASEAN, but only 11.6 percent of China's exports to ASEAN (in 2000). The commodities that China enjoys the advantage are: base metal and metal articles, textile and apparel and footwear, vegetable products and prepared foodstuffs, vehicles, stone/cement/ceramics and miscellaneous manufactured articles. They account for 38 percent of China's exports to ASEAN but only 8.8 percent of China's imports from ASEAN (in 2000). The second category of commodities include chiefly machinery and electrical appliances, chemicals, optical, precision & musical instruments, etc. Among them, machinery and electrical appliances account for 39 percent of China's exports to ASEAN and 41 percent of China's imports from ASEAN. The machinery and electrical appliances exported by China to ASEAN are mostly those for general or special use, but a substantial part of the machinery and electrical appliances China imports from ASEAN are electronic components and devices. For example, of the US$2.88 billion worth of machinery and electrical alliances that China imported from Malaysia, more than half of them were kinescopes, transistors and integrated circuits with more than 40 percent machinery and electrical appliances. Transistors, integrated circuits and other electronic components and devices accounted for a high percentage of China's import of machinery and electrical appliances from the

Philippines, Singapore and Thailand. This indicates that, in China–ASEAN trade, ASEAN's advantage in machinery and electrical appliances is mainly centered on electronic components and devices like integrated circuits, while China has certain advantage in general-use and special machinery and electrical appliances.

The Chinese economy's sustained and stable development is the main contributing factor in the recent development of China–ASEAN bilateral trade. Future potential is promising. However, the structure of China–ASEAN trade still remains at a relatively low stage, and a close industrial division of labor between the two sides has not been established. The basis of their current bilateral trade is largely on the complementarity of their material resources though the share of capital-intensive and technology-intensive products is rising. In China–ASEAN trade over the years, the proportion of trade linked to investment has been growing. It should be noted for manufactured goods that a large part of these is evidently influenced by the multinational corporations (MNCs) in their strategic investment allocation and operation in the region. For example, most of the electronic components exported by ASEAN are products of foreign-owned enterprises. China has a large amount of FDI from MNCs. The high proportion of FDI-related foreign trade in China's total foreign trade — which will strengthen in future, will have a significant influence on China–ASEAN bilateral trade in the future since they are linked by a regional network of MNCs.

China's entry into WTO will provide new opportunities for China–ASEAN trade relations, especially in China increasing its imports from ASEAN. It will prompt a major adjustment in the country's economic structure and will also influence the region in a similar adjustment. There may emerge a new structure of division of labor in the region which may offer an even more stable basis for the development of China–ASEAN economic relations.

China will increase its import of products of material resources from ASEAN. Being rich in material resources, ASEAN complements China perfectly and will be an important source for China to expand import of material resources. China will increase its import of intermediate products from ASEAN. After entering WTO, the export of labor-intensive products from China will increase. But China's labor-intensive industries are also raw material- and intermediate-product-intensive industries. In China's textile and light industries, the proportion of raw materials accounts for more than 75 percent of their cost, and the workers' wages, only seven percent.[9] Likewise, the exports of China's processing trade, which engages itself mainly in producing labor-intensive products, accounts for half of the country's total export, but it also needs to import large quantities of intermediate products. Especially in the textile and garment sectors, the intermediate products to be imported account for about 95 percent of their total imports.[10] Therefore, expansion of China's export of labor-intensive products will lead to sustainable growth of its import of related raw materials and intermediate products.

With new industrial adjustments in China and East Asia region, as well as corresponding allocation of FDI, it is expected that China and ASEAN can establish a new and close relationship of the division of labor. East Asia's capital flow before the financial crisis was targeted mainly at places of low-cost production and the products were mainly exported to markets outside the region. In the new industrial readjustment, China may engage itself in developing some new industries and new products instead of duplicating the existing industries of East Asia. Thus, it would be possible to mitigate the similarity between the industrial structures of China and ASEAN and hence to enlarge the room for division of labor as well as cooperation between the two sides.

With accession to the WTO, China will be a more powerful driver of growth. It has significant implications for China's trading partners. The ASEAN countries benefited largely from China's

---

[9] Shi Qingqi *et al.* (ed.) (2000). *Development Report of China's Industries 2000*. China Light Industries Publishing House, p. 27.
[10] Yu Yongding *et al.* (ed.) (2000). *The Research Report on China's Entry into WTO*. Social Sciences Documentation Publishing House, p. 55.

phenomenal growth in 1990s since China's imports from ASEAN have grown faster than from the rest of the world. By accession to the WTO, China will increase its gross imports by a rather big margin and will simultaneously restrain the development of some of its own industries whose products will be replaced by imports from abroad. Among these products, the following are relevant to ASEAN: rice, palm oil, rubber, chemicals, textiles, pulp and paper, petroleum products, telecommunications, machinery and electrical appliances, grain and oil processing products, etc. It is estimated that after WTO accession, China's import will grow at an average annual rate of 10 percent. On the basis of this estimation, China's imports from ASEAN is forecast to amount to US$35.5 billion in 2005, an increase of US$13.3 billion from the present, of which about US$4 billion will result from China's entry into WTO. With a good record in the 1990s of a higher average annual growth rate of China's imports from ASEAN (21 percent) than its gross imports from the world (15 percent), it is expected that this tendency will most probably continue, i.e. the growth rate of China's imports from ASEAN will continue to exceed that of its gross imports, and the actual volume of China's imports from ASEAN will continue to be bigger than what has been forecast eariler.

Among all the commodities imported by China in 2000, ASEAN can enjoy comparative advantage[11] of six categories (according to the HS), including animal and vegetable oils, mineral products, plastics and rubber, wood articles, pulp and paper, machinery and electrical appliances. These commodities were then valued at US$18.4 billion and accounted for 83 percent of China's imports from ASEAN. China's gross import during the period from 1993 to 2000, except for animal and vegetable oils, the import of all the above-mentioned commodities grew at an average annual rate of 14.7 percent, obviously surpassing that of the growth of

---

[11] $Pi = SMi/Tmi$. $Pi > 1$ means a category enjoying comparative advantage; SMi means the proportion of products of the "i" category in China's imports from ASEAN; TMi means the proportion of products of the "i" category in China's gross imports.

China's gross imports (11.7 percent). This shows that these products were the main items of China's imports. According to some studies on the possible changes in China's imports after its entry into WTO, these products will still be among the items for expanded import.

Chemicals belong to a category of products which ASEAN enjoys a potential advantage, and their proportion in China's imports will possibly increase along with their development in future. Among all of China's imports from ASEAN are some items of which ASEAN enjoys a comparative advantage, such as miscellaneous chemicals (accounting for 1.5 percent); there are also some items of material resources, such as fruits, coffee, cocoa, amylum, vegetables and their products, vegetable plaiting materials, grain, sugar and spices (accounting for 2.2 percent). Besides, there are some items of which ASEAN has a potential advantage[12] (totally accounting for about 7.5 percent), including organic chemicals, lubricants, dyes, chemical fibers, etc. (subtotally accounting for 5.1 percent), and copper and their products, glass and glassware (subtotally accounting for 1.7 percent). In sum, all the chemicals imported by China from ASEAN are valued at nearly US$6.65 billion (accounting for 1.5 percent). It is expected that China will also see a rapid rise in its import of chemicals from ASEAN.

China's products which enjoy an advantage in the ASEAN market are chiefly: textiles and garments, footwear, food, grains, building materials, and miscellaneous products. These products account for 21 percent ASEAN's gross imports from China in 1999. Judging from the developments in the 1990s, which witnessed a rather high rate of growth of ASEAN's import of most of these products from China, it should be possible for China to maintain its advantageous position in the ASEAN market in the coming years. China's products enjoying potential advantage on the ASEAN market are mainly: machinery and electrical appliances, optical instruments/clocks/watches, means of transports, metal

---

[12] This paper defines the products enjoying comparative advantage as follows: $0.5 < Pi < 1$.

products and chemicals. These products account for 70 percent of ASEAN's gross imports from China, among which machinery and electrical appliances alone account for 51.5 percent in 1999. During the period from 1993 to 1999, ASEAN rapidly increased its import of these products from China, at a growth rate much higher than that of ASEAN's gross import of these products from the rest of the world. Therefore, it can be expected that China's share in the ASEAN market will continue to grow.

China's entry into WTO will evidently not increase the pressure on developing countries like ASEAN member states for export competition. China will engage itself in a new round of adjustment and upgrading of its industrial structure after its entry into WTO, i.e., to develop some new industries and expand their market share instead of simply duplicating the existing industries of some relatively advanced countries. As a result, China's export will continue to grow and the country will reduce possible direct collisions with countries of similar development levels.

USA, Japan and EU are the three major export markets for both China and ASEAN. ASEAN's share in these three markets decreased from 5.6 percent in 1996 to 5.5 percent in 1999 while China's share increased from 4.2 percent to 5.4 percent in the same period.[13] They are now basically on par with each other. The main reasons why ASEAN's share has remained stagnant in these markets are the decrease in Japan's imports and the decline of ASEAN's own export capability as a result of the financial crisis. The structure of ASEAN's products exported to the three major markets mentioned above is too monotonous, and therefore, weak. The problem is most conspicuous on the American market. Among the American imports from ASEAN in 1999, machinery and electrical appliances accounted for as much as 62.2 percent; next came textiles and garments, nine percent; and the third was miscellaneous products, 3.1 percent. By contrast, the percentages of other categories of products were all lower than three percent (according to the HS system). The structure of EU's imports from ASEAN is similar. Such

---

[13] United Nations HS COMTRADE Data.

a lopsided structure of exports is evidently vulnerable to outside impact, and certainly not something to be easily affected by China.

With its WTO accession, China may see an obvious growth in its export of textiles and garments, but that will not necessarily affect foreign trade of China and ASEAN in other international markets in respect of these products, notwithstanding the fact that textiles and garments are the second biggest category of ASEAN's exports to USA and EU. In the USA's import of textiles and garments, China's share decreased from 16.1 percent in 1993 to 11.2 percent in 1999 while ASEAN's share decreased from 11.8 percent to 10.4 percent. And in the EU's import of these products in the same period, the shares of China and ASEAN both rose a little. Obviously, in the American and European textile and garment markets in the 1990s, there was no trade-off effects between Chinese products and ASEAN's products since ASEAN basically maintained its share in the American and European markets. The main reason for the decrease of the shares held by China and ASEAN was the impact of the NAFTA. It is noted that the main beneficiary of the NAFTA is Mexico, whose export of garments grew at an average annual rate of 33 percent in the 1990s and which has finally replaced China's first place in USA's import of garments.[14]

IV. Impact to FDI Flow

FDI grew rapidly in the 1990's. From 1987 to 1992, the world annual average flow of FDI was about US$173.5 billion, and it surged to US$865.4 billion in 1999. The FDI flowing into Asian developing countries also increased to US$105.6 billion in 1999 from US$54.8 billion in 1993, even though its percentage of the world FDI declined to 12 percent in 1999 from 27 percent in 1994.

Both China and ASEAN were large FDI recipients before the East Asian financial crisis. The annual average FDI flow into China and ASEAN in 1987–1992 was US$4.6 billion and US$9.5 billion

---

[14] WTO (2000). *International Trade Statistics 2000*, p. 152.

respectively, soaring to US$41.7 billion and US$27.6 billion in 1996 respectively. The economies had been keeping high growth rates before 1997. High expectation of investment return in these booming economies was the main impetus of FDI. ASEAN was considered to be one of the most profitable markets for investors. China adopted a "pro-FDI policy" after its reform and "opening-up." Due to its large population and economic dynamics, China's huge domestic market potential became a magnet for FDI.

The financial crisis significantly changed the economic environment of the region for FDI flow. Because of economic difficulty and also political instability, FDI flow into ASEAN countries has decreased sharply since 1997. The proportion of ASEAN countries' FDI inflow in all developing countries and Asian developing countries declined from 20 percent and 32 percent in 1996 to 11 percent and 20 percent in 1998 respectively, and further to eight percent and 15 percent in 1999. The confidence of foreign investors was significantly eroded by economic turmoil and social uncertainty, which is the main reason for declining FDI inflow to the ASEAN region. Almost all ASEAN countries experienced sharp decrease of FDI inflow after the financial crisis. FDI to Thailand had a short recovery in 1998 because of banking re-capitalization, but began to decrease from 1999. FDI flow into Malaysia was US$7.3 billion in 1996, and decreased more than half to only US$3.5 billion in 1999. FDI flow to Singapore in 1998 decreased 39 percent compared with 1996, and did not return to pre-crisis levels until 1999. FDI into Vietnam also experienced a steep decline. Because of great economic and political difficulties, FDI flow to Indonesia was even negative for many years.

At the same time, the impact of the financial crisis on China appeared to be slight. From 1997–2000, the average annual FDI to China exceeded US$40 billion, though, for example, real inflow in 1999 showed a 11 percent decline compared to that in 1997.[15] However, because of China's continuous high economic growth and stable financial situation after the financial crisis, it became the most attractive market for FDI allocation.

---

[15] *China Statistical Yearbook*, 2000.

As a matter of fact, the great potential of China's domestic market is a fundamental impetus for FDI inflow. China's GDP reached US$1 trillion in 2000. China's domestic market of one-fifth of the world's population is the natural focus of FDI. Market-seeking FDI products, such as automobile, mobile phone, detergent and cosmetics, etc. have increased remarkably. For example, China's mobile phone users exceeded 100 million in the first half of 2001 which encouraged major mobile phone makers, like Motorola, Ericsson and Nokia to further increase their investment in China. China's entry into WTO has clearly become a new factor in attracting FDI. The commitments made by China, such as opening up telecommunication, finance, insurance, and services, would provide more opportunities for FDI to flow into those sectors that used to be protected.

Great concern has been raised about the impact of FDI flow to China on other developing countries, especially ASEAN. China is regarded as a competitor of ASEAN in attracting foreign investments. Seemingly, the facts support the concern since the positive trend and big amounts of FDI flow into China are in contrast to the declining trend and reduced amounts to ASEAN countries. Nevertheless, in a detailed analysis, there appears no direct trade-off between FDI flow to China and to ASEAN. Judging from the trends before the financial crisis, both FDI flow to China and ASEAN increased significantly. The contraction of FDI to ASEAN in recent years is clearly a result of the negative impact of the financial crisis.

FDI flow to China has been steadily increasing since the early 1990s. However, before the financial crisis, the rate of FDI increment in ASEAN was faster than that in China. The declining confidence of foreign investment in East Asia caused by the financial crisis has decreased the share of FDI flow into developing countries on a large scale, while that to developed countries has shown a significant increase. In fact, the contraction of FDI to ASEAN was caused not just by the decrease in investment from developed countries, but also by sharp decline of intra-ASEAN investment. Clearly, general deterioration of the economic as well as political environment in ASEAN is the major cause of the reduction of FDI flow into the region. The positive trend of FDI flow to ASEAN will be resumed once the economic and political environments improve.

Furthermore, the latest increment of FDI into China is coming mostly from Europe and the US, as well as Taiwan. With strong market-seeking strategy, such investments from Europe and the US will probably not move to ASEAN, even if they were not moving to China. That is to say, investments to China and to ASEAN are generally based on different strategies, meaning that FDI to China may not create a clear or strong substitutive effect on ASEAN. With liberalization of the market following China's accession to WTO, investors may find not just ASEAN's internal market potential (due to AFTA), but also ASEAN's advantage in producing goods and exporting them to China.

With enhancement of its economic strength and also the need of industrial restructuring, China's investment abroad will surely increase. Currently, most of China's FDI to other countries are resource-related, i.e. for meeting its increasing resource demand. However, China will invest more in capital-intensive productions in the areas of electrical and electronic products. Increasing numbers of successful Chinese companies producing color TVs, refrigerator, washing machine, etc, have already set up factories in Africa, Latin America, Eastern Europe and Russia though the total amount of investments is not very big. FDI abroad by Chinese companies is encouraged by Chinese government policy.

ASEAN is not yet a major market for China's FDI with only less than US$100 million a year. Most of the investments go to four ASEAN new members, i.e., Vietnam, Laos, Cambodia and Myanmar. However, ASEAN will be one of the best potential markets for China's FDI outflow in the future, especially if a closer economic relationship between the two parties can be established. This will encourage more Chinese companies to invest in ASEAN countries.

Most ASEAN countries have abundant resources. With China's fast growing demand for resources, Chinese companies will be interested in the resource-developing and -processing industry in

ASEAN. AFTA will significantly drop tariff rates within ASEAN. Chinese companies will find themselves in a more favorable position if they produce locally. Due to geographical linkage and historical advantage, the southern part of China will form closer economic integration with ASEAN members which will surely attract more investments from China. With increase of FDI between China and ASEAN, either trade-led investment or investment-led trade will develop significantly, which will not only grow trade faster, but also change the structure of the trade. Although trade between China and ASEAN now accounts for a low proportion on both sides' external trade, and investment from and to either side is marginal, the potential is considerable. A FTA-based China–ASEAN economic linkage will turn them into a vast barrier-free region that helps to rationalize the economic activities between China and ASEAN. It is expected that close economic integration between China and ASEAN can bring mutual benefits and will play an important role in building up economic dynamism for both sides.

CHAPTER FOURTEEN

China–ASEAN FTA and Its Impact[1]

I. Why China–ASEAN FTA Started First?

Why did China initiate a FTA with ASEAN first? The simple answer is that it is easier to be realized. This simple answer contains three aspects: First, considering the East Asian cooperation process, it is difficult to realize an East Asian FTA (EAFTA) in a short time, though the benefits from EAFTA would be much larger than CAFTA. The practical approach is to start with the easier route first, which may play a stimulus role in facilitating the EAFTA. Second, China and ASEAN have increasingly shared interests in their trade and economic relations. Third, they have a similar strategy in promoting regional integration and cooperation. This shows that the China–ASEAN FTA meets their mutual interests, and is part of the grand strategy for both sides in promoting East Asian integration and cooperation.

For China, a FTA with ASEAN can be an experiment in participating and promoting regional integration and cooperation since joining the WTO. China is more confident of making a FTA with ASEAN since it shares great similarity with ASEAN countries. Political gains are also important for China since a closer economic

---

[1] Paper was presented at Japan Study Group Conference on East Asian FTA in 2003, Tokyo, Japan.

relationship helps to smooth comprehensive relations between them which will be significant in creating a peaceful environment for China.

For ASEAN, China's entry into WTO has raised great concern since China would become more competitive and attractive to foreign investors. At the same time, ASEAN also seeks for opportunities in a more liberalized and prosperous Chinese market through integrating with China. Being open to the competition puts positive pressure on ASEAN to facilitate its internal reform.

The concern on China's WTO accession was raised by the ASEAN leaders during the "10+3" summit in Singapore in 2000. China proposed a joint study for a long-term China–ASEAN close economic arrangement. The study made a positive conclusion for a FTA and a comprehensive economic partnership between China and ASEAN. The study pointed out that the establishment of a free trade arrangement (FTA) between ASEAN and China "will create the largest FTA, made up of developing countries, in terms of population, GDP and trade. The removal of trade barriers between ASEAN and China will lower costs, increase intra-regional trade and increase economic efficiency." The FTA will lead to greater specialization in production based on comparative advantage. Trade creation occurs when some domestic production in one FTA member is replaced by lower-cost imports from another member. This will boost real income in both regions as resources flow to sectors where they can be more efficiently and productively utilized. The simulations conducted by the ASEAN Secretariat using the Global Trade Analysis Project (GTAP) suggest that an ASEAN–China FTA will increase ASEAN's exports to China by 48 percent and China's exports to ASEAN by 55.1 percent. The FTA increases ASEAN's GDP by 0.9 percent or by US$ 5.4 billion while China's real GDP expands by 0.3 percent or by US$ 2.2 billion in absolute terms.

The study found that the formation of an ASEAN–China FTA should also attract more investments into the region. The integration of ASEAN with China can entice more foreign corporations, which each market alone cannot otherwise attract. With a larger market, more intense competition, increased investment and economies of scale, enterprises will invest more in research and development, hence promoting technological innovation.

The significance of a FTA between China and ASEAN will go beyond economic gain. "It will help to create community between ASEAN members and China. Their geographic closeness, long historical ties and shared culture lay a good foundation for further cooperation. The sense of community engendered by an ASEAN–China FTA will contribute immensely to peace and stability in the Asia Pacific region."[2]

This positive conclusion encouraged the leaders of China and ASEAN to agree on a strategy to establish a FTA between the two sides within 10 years in 2001 and to sign the framework document for a comprehensive close economic partnership in 2002.

II. China–ASEAN Relations in Progress

China and ASEAN have become important trade partners. Currently, ASEAN is China's fifth largest trade partner, and China is ASEAN's sixth largest partner. Since the late 1980s, the average annual growth rate in trade between ASEAN and China has been more than 20 percent. China's export to ASEAN increased from US$4.1 billion in 1991 to US$18.4 billion in 2001, and its import from ASEAN increased from US$3.8 billion in 1991 to US$23.2 billion in 2001. Most of China–ASEAN trade goods are manufactured products. In 2001, 70.6 percent of China's imports and 84.9 percent of exports are manufactured goods. Based on the new network of FDI in the region, China will import more manufactured parts from ASEAN (see Figures 1 and 2).

ASEAN is one of the major FDI sources for China. By the end of 2001, FDI from ASEAN to China reached US$25.2 billion, accounting for 6.6 percent of total FDI flow into China.[3] However, China's

---

[2] A Report submitted to the ASEAN–China Expert Group on Economic Cooperation by Joint Research Team on 27 September 2001.

[3] ASEAN accounts for 11 percent of FDI flow to China in 1997, only 4.9 percent in 2001 due to the impact of the financial crisis.

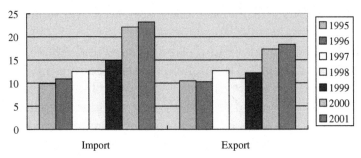

Source: Statistics for China–ASEAN Trade, 2002, MOFTEC.

Figure 1: China's trade with ASEAN (1995–2001).

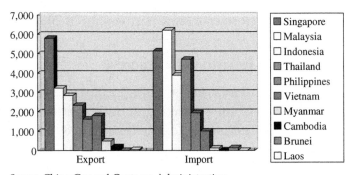

Source: China General Customs Administration.

Figure 2: China's trade with ASEAN members in 2001.

investment in ASEAN is still small compared to ASEAN investment in China, only US$0.65 billion by the end of 2001. But it is expected that China's investment in ASEAN will increase significantly in the coming years. Besides, China has large contracted projects in ASEAN with a total value of US$12.4 billion by the end of 2001.

China's entry into WTO will provide both challenges and opportunities to China–ASEAN relations. For challenges, China will produce more and more cheaper and high-quality goods based on cheap labor and increasing FDI flow with easier access to foreign markets. Due to China's unique market potential, China is more attractive than ASEAN for large FDI flow. For opportunity, China will provide a larger market for ASEAN, not just in material resources, but also manufactured goods based on a kind of "network production division." In recent years, China has already significantly increased import of intermediate products from ASEAN. As a matter of fact, China's labor-intensive industries are also raw material and intermediate product-intensive industries. Thus, China also needs to import large quantities of intermediate products. Even in the textile and garment sectors, intermediate products that need to be imported account for about 95 percent of their total imports.[4] Therefore, the expansion of China's export of labor-intensive products may lead to sustainable growth of its import of related raw materials and intermediate products.

With new industrial adjustments in China and the East Asian region, as well as corresponding allocation of FDI, it is expected that China and ASEAN can establish a new and close relationship of division of labor. It would be possible to mitigate the similarity between the industrial structures of China and ASEAN and hence enlarge the room for division of labor as well as cooperation between the two sides.

China will be a more powerful driver of growth. This has significant implications for China's trading partners. The ASEAN countries benefited largely from China's phenomenal growth in 1990s since China's imports from ASEAN have grown faster than from the rest of the world. With economic growth, China will increase its gross imports by a rather big margin. Among these products, the following are relevant to ASEAN: rice, palm oil, rubber, chemicals, textiles, pulp and paper, petroleum products, telecommunications, machinery and electrical appliances, grain and oil processing products, etc. It is estimated that China's import will grow at an average annual rate of 10 percent in general, but at a much higher growth rate from ASEAN. The trade figure of 2002 showed that China has become ASEAN's most promising market for export. ASEAN has become the fourth largest partner for China's import after Japan, Taiwan and EU. This reflects a

---

[4] Yu Yongding *et al.* (ed.) (2000). *The Research Report on China's Entry into WTO*. Social Sciences Documentation Publishing House, p. 55.

fact that ASEAN can benefit significantly from an economically booming China.

China's economic growth and increasing competition will bring about challenges to ASEAN countries. But, this should not be exaggerated since "unrestricted surge of China's exports are unlikely owing to the existence of specific provisions."[5] Moreover, China will engage itself in a new round of adjustment and upgrading of its industrial structure i.e., to develop some new industries and expand their market share instead of simply duplicating the existing industries of some relatively advanced countries. As a result, China's foreign trade will continue to grow and it will be able to reduce possible direct collisions with countries of similar development levels.

Both China and ASEAN were large FDI recipients before the East Asian financial crisis. The annual average FDI flow into China and ASEAN in 1987–1992 was US$4.6 billion and US$9.5 billion respectively, soaring to US$41.7 billion and US$27.6 billion in 1996 respectively. The main factors attracting FDI are that the economies had been keeping high growth rates before 1997. High expectation of investment return in these booming economies was the main impetus of FDI. ASEAN was considered to be one of the most profitable markets for investors. China adopted a 'pro-FDI policy' after its reform and opening up. Due to its large population and economic dynamics, China's huge domestic market potential became a magnet attracting FDI.

The financial crisis significantly changed the economic environment of the region for FDI flow. The confidence of foreign investment was significantly eroded by economic turmoil and social uncertainty, which is the main reason for declining FDI inflow into ASEAN region. Almost all ASEAN countries experienced sharp decrease of FDI inflow after the financial crisis.

While at the same time, the impact of the financial crisis on China appeared to be slighter. Because of China's continuous high

---

[5] Hong Kong Trade Development Council (2002). China's accession to WTO: Embracing the Opportunities, Meeting the Challenges.

economic growth and stable financial situation after the financial crisis, it becomes the most attractive market for FDI allocation. Great potential of China's domestic market is a fundamental impetus for FDI inflow. China's GDP per capita reached to 1000 US dollars in 2001. The entry into WTO will bring about significant positive impact to China's future economic growth. Market-seeking products of FDI, such as automobile, mobile phone, detergent and cosmetics, etc. have increased remarkably. China's entry into WTO has clearly become a new factor in attracting FDI. The commitments made by China, such as opening up telecom-munication, finance, insurance, and services, would provide more opportunities for FDI to flow into those sectors that used to be protective. However, with strong market-seeking strategy, invest-ments to China and to ASEAN are generally based on different strategies. This shows that based on the rational arrangements, FDI to China should not create a clear or strong substitutive effect to ASEAN.

With enhancement of its economic strength and also the need of industrial restructuring, China's investment abroad will surely increase. Currently, most of China's FDI to other countries are resource related, i.e. for meeting its increasing resource demand. However, China will invest more in capital-intensive productions in the areas of electrical and electronic products. Increasing number of Chinese successful companies in color TV set, refrigerator, washing machine, etc, have already set up their factories in Africa, Latin America, Eastern Europe and Russia though total amount of the investments are still not very big.

ASEAN is expected to become an attractive market for China's FDI overseas strategy. ASEAN may be one of the most potential markets for China's FDI flow in the future, especially if a closer economic relationship between the two sides can be established. There will be some factors, which will play important role in pushing China's investment into ASEAN in the future. Most ASEAN countries have abundant resources. With fast growing of China's demand for resources, Chinese companies will be interested in the resource developing and processing industry in ASEAN.

AFTA will make significant drop in tariff rates within ASEAN. Chinese companies will find themselves in a more favored position if they produce locally.

Due to geographical linkage and advantage, Southern part of China will form closer economic integration with ASEAN members, like Vietnam, Laos, Cambodia and Myanmar, even Thailand, which will surely attract more investments from China. With increase of FDI between China and ASEAN, either trade-led investment or investment-led trade will be developed, which will not only make trade grow faster, but also change the structure of the trade.

III. Implications of China–ASEAN FTA

At a Summit held in Brunei on 6 November 2001, the leaders of ASEAN and China agreed to establish a Free Trade Area within 10 years. Aside from the FTA, the leaders also agreed to strengthen cooperation in the fields of agriculture, information and communication technologies, human resources development, mutual investment and the Great Mekong River development. The framework agreement was signed in November of 2002 during the leaders' meeting in Cambodia, which represents remarkable progress in implementing the leaders' decision for a China–ASEAN FTA and other economic cooperation.

1. *What does the framework agreement cover?*

The signed framework agreement set up important principles for the China–ASEAN FTA process. As stated, the aim of the China–ASEAN FTA is "to minimize barriers and deepen economic linkages between the parties; lower costs; increase intra-regional trade and investment; increase economic efficiency; create a larger market with greater opportunities and larger economies of scale for the businesses of the parties; and enhance the attractiveness of the parties to capital and talent"; and "to create a partnership between the parties, and provide an important mechanism for strengthening co-operation and supporting economic stability in East Asia."[6] The coverage of liberalization through FTA is comprehensive, including goods, services and also investments. According to the framework agreement, the FTA will be realized through "progressive elimination of tariffs and non-tariff barriers in substantially all trade in goods; progressive liberalization of trade in services with substantial sectoral coverage; establishment of an open and competitive investment regime that facilitates and promotes investment within the ASEAN–China FTA."[7]

Given the internal differences of ASEAN, liberalization will be done on different tracks and different timetables. For the trade in goods, the normal track will be implemented with specified schedules and rates from 1 January 2005 to 2010 for ASEAN 6 and China, and in the case of the newer ASEAN Member States, from 1 January 2005 to 2015 with higher starting tariff rates and at different stages. The sensitive track will be in accordance with the mutually agreed end rates and end dates, and "where applicable, have their respective applied MFN tariff rates progressively eliminated within timeframes to be mutually agreed between the parties."[8]

For liberalization of trade in services, it will have substantial sectoral coverage and aim at "progressive elimination of substantially all discrimination between or among the parties and/or prohibition of new or more discriminatory measures with respect to trade in services between the parties." This liberalization aims at "expansion in the depth and scope of liberalisation of trade in services beyond those undertaken by ASEAN member states and China under the GATS, and enhanced co-operation in services between the parties in order to improve efficiency and competitiveness, as well as to diversify the supply and distribution of services of the respective service suppliers of the parties."

---

[6] Framework Agreement, 4 November 2002, p. 2.
[7] Framework Agreement, 4 November 2002, p. 3.
[8] Framework Agreement, 4 November 2002, p. 6.

Investment liberalization is "to promote investments and to create a liberal, facilitative, transparent and competitive investment regime, "to strengthen co-operation in investment, facilitate investment and improve transparency of investment rules and regulations and to provide for the protection of investments."[9]

The framework agreement set the specific timetables for the negotiations of the FTA, i.e. the final negotiation to be finished by June of 2004. Based on the solid foundation of the preparation, it seems reasonable to be optimistic of this conclusion.

An important part of the framework agreement is the early harvest program (EHP). It is considered as a remarkable progress of the FTA establishment and also the good will of the two sides since it was mutually agreed by consultation rather than negotiation. EHP considers the differences of ASEAN members and makes different arrangements for sensitive goods of exemption, and also different timeframes for different categories. According to the framework agreement, Category 1, for China and ASEAN 6, refers to all products with applied MFN tariff rates higher than 15 percent; for the newer ASEAN member states, this refers to all products with applied MFN tariff rates of 30 percent or higher. Category 2, for China and ASEAN 6, refers to all products with applied MFN tariff rates between five percent (inclusive) and 15 percent (inclusive); for the newer ASEAN member states, it refers to all products with applied MFN tariff rates between 15 percent (inclusive) and 30 percent (exclusive). Category 3, for China and ASEAN 6, refers to all products with applied MFN tariff rates lower than five percent; for the newer ASEAN member states, it refers to all products with applied MFN tariff rates lower than 15 percent.[10] EHP will be implemented from 1 January 2004 and to be fully realized in 2006. This is unique in any FTA negotiation.

FTA is just one core part of the framework agreement. Also listed are other areas for broad cooperation. Five areas are listed as priority sectors for cooperation: agriculture; information and

---

[9] Framework Agreement, 4 November 2002, p. 8.
[10] Framework Agreement, 4 November 2002, p. 36.

communications technology; human resources development; investment; and Mekong River basin development. The co-operation will be extended to other areas including banking, finance, tourism, industrial co-operation, transport, telecommunications, intellectual property rights, small and medium enterprises (SMEs), environment, biotechnology, fishery, forestry and forestry products, mining, energy and sub-regional development. Measures to strengthen co-operation shall include: (a) Promotion and facilitation of trade in goods and services, and investment, such as standards and conformity assessment, technical barriers to trade/non-tariff measures, and customs co-operation; (b) Increasing the competitiveness of SMEs; (c) Promotion of electronic commerce; (d) Capacity-building; (e) Technology-transfer.

In order to adjust their economic structure and expand their trade and investment with China, capacity-building programmes and technical assistance, particularly for the newer ASEAN member states will be implemented.

Other areas for economic cooperation also include: (a) Acceleration of the implementation of the Singapore–Kunming Rail Link and Bangkok–Kunming Highway projects under the framework of ASEAN Mekong Basin Development Cooperation (AMBDC) and the Greater Mekong Sub-region (GMS) Programme respectively; (b) Implementation of the mid-term and long-term plans for the all-round development of the Greater Mekong Sub region (GMS); (c) Facilitation and promotion, through specific procedures and mechanisms to be developed, of trade and investment between the two sides; (d) Developing the mutual recognition arrangements in areas of mutual interests, for example, agricultural products, electronic and electrical equipment, and to be completed within agreed timeframes; (e) Establishment of co-operation mechanism between standards and conformity authorities to enhance trade facilitation and co-operation in other areas; (f) Cooperation in information and communications technology sector; (g) Development of specific programmes for cooperation in human resources development; (h) Establishment of specific technical programmes to assist the newer ASEAN member states to build their capacity for regional integration and facilitation of the WTO accession process of the non-WTO ASEAN member states; (i) Establishment of cooperation mechanism between customs authorities to enhance trade facilitation; (j) Establishment of cooperation mechanism in the field of intellectual property rights protection.

Considering the special importance of agricultural cooperation between China and ASEAN, a memorandum of understanding on agricultural cooperation was signed separately at the same time. Some specific areas for cooperation were identified, such as training on hybrid rice, cultivation skills, fertilizer and water management, aquaculture specialists, biotechnology application in agriculture, farm machinery, agro–industry, agricultural extension, livestock, as well as technology in agriculture, forestry, post-harvest technology, and food security.[11]

Nevertheless, this does not mean the framework agreement has solved everything. Much remain to be done in the process of negotiation which has to be concluded by June of 2004.

2. *Beyond economic cooperation*

Economic integration and cooperation needs a good political environment and strong political support. China–ASEAN political relations have gradually improved since the 1990s through bilateral relations and also East Asian regional cooperation process. In order to strengthen the political foundation of the FTA and comprehensive economic cooperation, China and ASEAN signed two other documents: one is on cooperation in non-traditional security, another is on the code of conduct of the South China Sea.

The signing of the code of conduct is an important step of progress for the China–ASEAN political foundation since they declared "to resolve their territorial and jurisdictional disputes by

---

[11] Memorandum of Understanding on Agriculture Cooperation, 4 November 2002.

peaceful means, without resorting to the threat or use of force, through friendly consultations and negotiations by sovereign states directly concerned, in accordance with universally recognized principles of international law, including the 1982 UN Convention on the Law of the Sea" and "to exercise self-restraint in the conduct of activities that would complicate or escalate disputes and affect peace and stability including, among others, refraining from action of inhabiting on the presently uninhabited islands, reefs, shoals, cays, and other features and to handle their differences in a constructive manner." This does not provide a mechanism for releasing tensions, but may provide opportunity for possible cooperation such as "marine environmental protection; marine scientific research; safety of navigation and communication at sea; search and rescue operation."[12]

Economic integration and interdependence will help to build up political confidence. Both China and ASEAN realize the significance of their political relations. China's economic emergence and increasing influence have created big challenges for ASEAN, but are not a threat. A stable and cooperative relationship with its close neighbors is desirable for China to serve its grand strategy for a long-term peaceful environment for development.

3. *A dimension for East Asian cooperation*

China and ASEAN have moved ahead in forging FTA and comprehensive economic cooperation. Considering the great importance of the process of East Asian cooperation, the question is whether this would play a positive or a negative role.[13] From my perspective, it will play a positive role in encouraging other countries to formulate a free trade arrangement with ASEAN, or in pressing

---

[12] Declaration on conduct in the South China Sea, 4 November 2002.
[13] "The challenge is to work out how they fit together in the regionalism portfolio." Christopher Findlay and Mari Pangestu (2001). Regional trade arrangements in East Asia: where are they taking us? Paper presented at PECC Trade Policy Forum symposium, Bangkok, Thailand, p. 20.

China, ROK and Japan to facilitate their free trade arrangements on the one hand, and to facilitate the process of an East Asian FTA and community-building on the other hand. In the early stages of East Asian integration and cooperation, a kind of "competitive liberalization" through different arrangements by different parties is unavoidable. However, the integrated process of East Asian integration and cooperation under the framework of "10+3" is currently underway and considered to be the main course for the region which can play an important role in preventing different efforts from dividing the region into small blocks.

It is true that China–ASEAN FTA will help to create a big market based on preferential arrangements among themselves. Trade and investment diversion will occur due to those internal preferences. But both China and ASEAN will develop close relations with other countries since they have high dependency on other markets. An East Asian FTA (EAFTA) will take a longer time than China–ASEAN FTA, but the latter may provide a good case for how managing differences among parties with great disparities would not just be a good experiment for forging EAFTA, but also for building the political foundation for the East Asian community in the long run.

CHAPTER FIFTEEN

Comparing China and Japan in Developing the Partnership with ASEAN[1]

Introduction

ASEAN has become a highly integrated region under the 1992 ASEAN Free Trade Agreement (AFTA) which promoted regional cooperation and integration. The Bali Concord II document, signed at the October 2003 ASEAN summit in Bali, Indonesia, is designed to lead ASEAN towards a more integrated community by further liberalizing regional trade.

China normalized relations with Southeast Asian countries in the early 1990s — before which economic linkages were very weak but since then China's trade with states in the region has been developing at a very fast pace. Of significance in this connection are the ASEAN–China Framework Agreement on Comprehensive Economic Cooperation (CEC), signed in November 2002, and the document for a strategic partnership inked in 2003, both of which set a firm foundation for close economic and political cooperation.

Japan, the largest economy in East Asia, has been one of the most important economic players in ASEAN, providing an important market and investments considered key to the expansion of

---

[1] This paper was written for the conference organized by Japan Center for International Exchanges in 2004.

ASEAN's manufacturing industry. Nevertheless, due to its stagnant economy, Japan's trade with and investment in ASEAN have been declining. Tokyo is making every effort to strengthen its relations with the grouping's member states through a variety of arrangements such as Closer Economic Relations (CER) arrangements, to better accommodate the needs of the changing environment.

Regionalism is emerging in East Asia, as can be seen from the ASEAN + 3 (China, Japan, and Republic of Korea) initiative focusing on monetary and financial cooperation, although regional free trade areas (FTAs) remain a multi-layered process. ASEAN is seeking, through the ASEAN Free Trade Area (AFTA, implemented in 1993), to break through individual states' protectionism and form an integrated market, and promote cooperation on foreign direct investment (FDI) and technology transfers.

China has become more actively engaged in matters of regional concern since joining the World Trade Organization (WTO) in 2001. One of its first subsequent steps was to sign an agreement on economic cooperation with ASEAN (at the November 2001 summit in Brunei), which included the decision to set up an FTA within 10 years. But beyond that and in the longer term, China has a strong interest in promoting a broader-based East Asian FTA and regional community.

Japan is a key factor in any regional arrangement. While it has moved in a new direction by initiating and concluding bilateral FTAs with states in the East and Southeast Asian region, Tokyo remains opposed to truly comprehensive arrangements at both the bilateral and regional levels because it is not willing to liberalize trade in agricultural products.[2] It seems that Japan still needs time to adopt an East Asian strategy for such agreements. Nevertheless, it is crucial that China and Japan should cooperate in helping to achieve East Asian integration and cooperation, given

---

[2] Drysdale, Peter and Kenichi Ishigaki (2001). *East Asian trade and financial integration: New issues*, Canberra: Asia-Pacific Press, p. 6.

their common interests in the economic benefits that would accrue. What is now required is the political will to work together based on a new consensus.

I. ASEAN Relations with China

From its initial small amount, China's trade with ASEAN is growing quickly and China is now an important trading partner of the group. Currently, ASEAN is China's fifth largest, and China is ASEAN's sixth largest trading partner. Since the early 1990s, China–ASEAN trade has been growing at an average annual rate of more than 20 percent, higher than the world average for the same period, and for most years since, China has had a trade deficit with its trading partners in the region.

ASEAN used to be one of the major sources of FDI into China, but the flow has slowed considerably since the 1997 financial crisis, accounting for 11 percent in 1997, and only 4.9 percent in 2001. Compared with what ASEAN has invested in China, China still invests relatively little in ASEAN, the figure having been US$0.65 billion for 2001. Nevertheless, China's investment in ASEAN is expected to increase significantly over the coming years. Besides, China has large contracted projects in ASEAN, the total value of which was more than US$12 billion by the end of 2001.

A striking development in China–ASEAN trade relations is that China has become a major market for ASEAN exports, as a result of which ASEAN member states have benefited hugely from China's phenomenal growth. China's imports from ASEAN have grown faster than those from the rest of the world. Moreover, as its economy expands, the trend is expected to continue. China's 1992 imports from ASEAN valued at US$5 billion had roughly doubled to US$10 billion by 1995, and the pattern was repeated when its 1999 imports worth US$15 billion more than doubled to US$30 billion in 2002. It is also worthy of note that, over the same 10-year period, China's exports to ASEAN member states also showed a sharp, albeit more restrained rise: from a value of US$5 billion in 1992 to US$10 billion in 1995, and from US$12 billion in 1999 to US$24 billion in 2002.[3]

The trade between China and ASEAN remains complementary, with China importing increasing amounts of such products as rice, palm oil, rubber, chemicals, textiles, pulp and paper, petroleum products, telecommunications equipment, machinery and electrical appliances, and grain and oil-processing products. Trade figures for 2002 show China to be ASEAN's most promising export market. In that year, China's imports from ASEAN marked a 26 percent year-on-year rise (representing a 10 percent share of its overall imports), a much greater increase than the 19 percent year-on-year growth in its imports from South Korea (9 percent), 14 percent year-on-year hike in imports from Japan (17 percent), and an eight percent (12 percent) and a four percent (14 percent) year-on-year climb in imports from Taiwan and the European Union respectively.[4] Furthermore, ASEAN is on the way to becoming China's fourth-largest source of imports after Japan, Taiwan, and the European Union. This is a good indication of the significant degree to which ASEAN can benefit from an economically booming China.

Until the Asian financial crisis of 1997, ASEAN was one of China's most important sources of FDI. ASEAN investment share in total FDI flow to China climbed steadily from some 5.5 percent in 1994 to 9.2 percent in 1997, after which the grouping's capacity to invest was greatly reduced and its share registered only 8 percent in 1999, 7 percent in 2000, and 6.2 percent in 2001.[5] Meanwhile, China's investment in ASEAN member states remains limited, the total amount up until 2001 having been less than $5 billion, although the potential seems promising should China's economic expansion continue.

---

[3] www.aseansec.org

[4] www.moftec.gov.cn

[5] *Yearbook of China Statistics*, 1995, 1997, 2002.

II. ASEAN Relations with Japan

Japan is ASEAN's second largest trading partner after the United States, and from 1993 until 2001, Japan–ASEAN two-way trade was almost equally distributed at about 15 percent of each party's total trade. In terms of Japan's imports from ASEAN member states over the nine-year period, the figure rose from US$21 billion in 1993 to US$35 billion in 1997, just prior to the financial crisis, after which it plummeted to US$25 billion in 1998 before rising to reach US$31 billion in 2001. Japan's exports to ASEAN followed a similar pattern, although the decline was not so sharp following the crisis, with exports figures settling at US$35 billion in 2001.[6]

However, Japan accounts for an increasingly declining share of ASEAN imports. From 25 percent of its total figure in 1993, ASEAN's imports from Japan rose to 26 percent in 1994 before sliding steadily to 16 percent of the total in 2001. The grouping's exports to Japan, meanwhile, dropped from 15 percent of its total export figure in 1993 to a low of 10 percent in 1999, after which it rose to settle at 12 percent in 2001.[7]

It should be noted that, between 1994 and the onset of the Asian financial crisis in 1997, ASEAN had a large trade deficit with Japan, but exported very little to China, although until 2001, China had imported almost the same amount as Japan from ASEAN member states. Then, between 1998 and 2001, China suddenly developed a trade deficit with ASEAN amounting to US$14.6 billion, while Japan recorded a trade surplus with ASEAN of close to US$23 billion.[8]

Japan has made substantial investments in ASEAN, accounting for 18.4 percent of the total FDI in ASEAN in 2001, and has played an important role in developing ASEAN's modern manufacturing industries, especially the export sector. Yet, even though ASEAN

---

[6] www.UNCTAD.org.
[7] www.UNCTAD.org.
[8] www.aseansec.org.

has long been a major destination for Japanese investments, they have begun to slow down over the last decade, as a result of which Japan's share of total investments in ASEAN has decreased from about 28 percent in 1991 to 18.4 percent in 2001.[9] Over the seven-year period from 1995 to 2001, Indonesia accounted for 25 percent of Japan's FDI in ASEAN; Thailand, for 23 percent; the Philippines, 21 percent; Vietnam, 14 percent; Singapore, 12 percent; and Malaysia, 11 percent; while Japanese FDI in Laos, Cambodia, and Myanmar is still marginal.[10] Its position vis-à-vis ASEAN has changed partly as a result of its economic difficulties, but also because of China's growing role in the region.

Both China and Japan have made great efforts to promote economic cooperation with ASEAN. Most of China's cooperation with the grouping commenced in the last decade of the 20th century has developed quickly since, while Japan–ASEAN cooperation began much earlier, slowed down after the financial crisis, and is now again being strengthened. Both China and Japan have emphasized that either a China–ASEAN FTA or a Japan–ASEAN CEP would go far in helping create an East Asian economic community.

III. China–ASEAN Cooperation

Cooperation between China and ASEAN dates back to 1991, when Chinese Foreign Minister Qian Qichen was invited to attend the opening session of the 24th ASEAN Ministerial Meeting in Kuala Lumpur, Malaysia, where he expressed interest in strengthening cooperation with ASEAN. In 1993, ASEAN and China agreed to establish two joint committees for cooperation in the areas of economics, trade, science, and technology. At the same time, ASEAN and China agreed to engage in consultations on political and security

---

[9] ASEAN–Japan Closer Economic Partnership (CEP); Joint Report of Japan-ASEAN experts group, 2003; ASEAN Secretariat.
[10] www.UNCTAD.org

issues of common concern at the ASEAN senior officials' level. In July 1996, China was accorded full dialogue partner status, and in 1997, China and ASEAN established the ASEAN–China Joint Cooperation Committee (ACJCC) and ASEAN–China Cooperation Fund (ACCF). In addition, China participates in several consultative meetings with ASEAN, including the ASEAN Regional Forum (ARF), the Post Ministerial Conference (PMC) 9 + 1 and 9 + 10, the Joint Cooperation Committee (JCC) meeting, the ASEAN–China Senior Officials Meeting (SOM) consultations, and the ASEAN–China Business Council Meeting.

At the Eighth ASEAN–China Summit in Phnom Penh on 4 November 2002, the comprehensive economic cooperation (CEC) agreement was signed, which provides the groundwork for the eventual establishment of an ASEAN–China Free Trade Area (FTA) by 2010 for the older ASEAN members and 2015 for the newer ones. Then in May 2002, the Trade Negotiating Committee (TNC) was established to negotiate a comprehensive agreement, and it is expected that negotiations for an FTA will be concluded by 30 June 2004. China–ASEAN cooperation has been expanding in five priority areas, namely, agriculture, information and communications technology, human resources development, two-way investment, and Mekong river basin development. Both parties also signed a Memorandum of Understanding on Agricultural Cooperation, which covers forestry, livestock production, fisheries, biotechnology, post-harvest technology, field harmonization of quarantine measures, and standards conformity of agriculture products.

Development cooperation has been progressing at a relatively fast pace, especially since the ASEAN–China Working Group on Development Cooperation (ACWGDC) was set up in May 2002, and includes the Greater Mekong Sub-Region (GMS), ASEAN Mekong Basin Development, and the Mekong River Commission frameworks. Between May 2002 and March 2003, ASEAN and China implemented 14 projects concerned with science and technology, information and communication technology (ICT), agriculture, transport, social development, human resources development, and mass media. More projects covering ICT, human resources development, science and technology, investment, transportation, academic exchanges, small and medium enterprises (SMEs), the environment, and cultural sectors are also expected to be implemented. In 2003, China and ASEAN signed a Memorandum of Understanding on Cooperation on Information and Communication Technology (www.aseansec.org). However, as a developing economy, China has played a very important role in assisting ASEAN economic development, although cooperation is still not what it could be were greater economic integration institutionalized.

But China–ASEAN cooperation extends beyond the economic area. In 2002, at the same time that the Framework Agreement on CEC was signed, the Joint Declaration of ASEAN and China on Cooperation in the Field of Non-Traditional Security Issues and the Declaration on the Conduct of Parties in the South China Sea were also adopted, with a view to promoting a peaceful and friendly environment in the South China Sea between ASEAN and China. In 2003, China formally signed the Treaty of Amity and Cooperation in Southeast Asia (TAC), a document sealing a strategic partnership that serves as a good foundation on which to improve political cooperation in the future. However, China–ASEAN cooperation and integration is not an easy goal to pursue, since it requires two vital ingredients: political will, and a deep pool of knowledge and mutual understanding.

IV. Japan–ASEAN Cooperation

Japan and ASEAN started their formal cooperation in 1977, when they decided to establish a forum for cooperation. In 1987, they announced a partnership designed to result in peace and prosperity, and then in 1997, Japanese Prime Minister Hashimoto Ryutaro announced his Hashimoto Doctrine that called for the development of partnerships and exchanges that were broader and deeper at the top and at all levels.

Over the years, Japan has participated in a series of consultative meetings with ASEAN, including the ASEAN Regional Forum (ARF), Post Ministerial Conference (PMC) 9 + 1 and 9 + 10, ASEAN Economic Ministers–Ministry of International Trade and Industry (AEM–MITI) consultations, ASEAN–Japan Forum, Senior Economic Officers–Ministry of International Trade and Industry (SEOM–MITI) consultations, Joint Planning Committee (JPC) meeting, ASEAN–Japan Economic Council (AJEC), and the ASEAN–Japanese Businessmen's Meeting (AJBM). The ASEAN–Tokyo Committee also assists in conducting and maintaining a dialogue with Japan, while regular dialogue meetings, such as the AEM–MITI Consultations and the ASEAN–Japan Forum, are now held annually, and Japan participates in ARF meetings.

In addition to being one of ASEAN's most important economic partners, Japan is a major contributor to development cooperation, having provided technical assistance through several programs, such as the Japan–ASEAN Cooperation Promotion Program (JACPP), the Intra-ASEAN Technical Exchange Program (IATEP), and the Japan–ASEAN Exchange Program (JAEP).

In 2002, Japanese Prime Minister Koizumi Junichiro visited a number of ASEAN countries and proposed the Koizumi Initiative, which comprises three pillars: filling economic gaps and enjoying prosperity, ensuring human dignity, and fostering democratic and stable governance (Kawaguchi, 2003).[11] He also proposed several initiatives for cooperation, including the designation of 2003 as the Year of ASEAN–Japan Exchange, the reinforcing of cooperation in the areas of education and human resources development, solidifying the security relations between Japan and ASEAN, and setting up an ASEAN–Japan CEP. The ASEAN–Japan Summit, held in Phnom Penh on November 5, 2002, issued a joint declaration endorsing the development of a framework for a comprehensive economic partnership to include elements that might be developed into an FTA. Here Japan was making every effort to reinforce its

---

[11] Kawaguchi Yoriko (2003). Building Bridges toward Our Future: Initiating for Reinforcing ASEAN Integration. Policy speech.

close relationship with ASEAN that had been negatively affected by the 1997 financial crisis and Japan's economic downturn.

When comparing the cooperation extended by China and Japan to ASEAN, it should be noted that, although Japan has a longer history than China of extending economic cooperation, and its role is greater, China seems to be moving faster than Japan in terms of promoting cooperation with ASEAN, and is offering broader programs aimed at achieving a working partnership.

China and Japan have different interests and strategies with regard to developing economic relations with ASEAN. Since some of the ASEAN member states are China's immediate neighbors, China not only shares an array of interests with them, but also tends to treat ASEAN as an integrated region. Stability in the region and a cooperative relationship will serve China's interests well in that a peaceful environment is crucial for its modernization. Although the China–ASEAN relationship is relatively new and rather different from the Japan–ASEAN ties characterized by a large and strategic regional market that Tokyo is hoping to further expand, there is potential for both China and Japan to interact more with ASEAN. In terms of East Asian regional cooperation, there are three particular areas in which greater interaction and cooperation would be possible.

V. China and Japan in the Region

Japanese FDI has created a large network of markets that are either within ASEAN, or outside the grouping but with which ASEAN member states conduct import and export business. As Japanese FDI in China has increased, so the network has developed into a Japan–China–ASEAN structure. Since the 1997 financial crisis, however, Japan has tended to allocate more FDI to China than to ASEAN states, the outcome of which has been a new China–ASEAN production network created by Japanese companies. The fast increase in ASEAN exports to China is a result of this new network of increasing exchanges of parts and components between Japanese investors in China and ASEAN.

This economic triangle has served to integrate the parties concerned more than ever before with, for example, ASEAN exports of computer components and machinery having risen from US$800 million in 1996 to US$1,900 million in 1998, before climbing to US$5,000 million in 1999, peaking at US$11,000 million in 2000, and then settling at US$9,000 million in 2001.

Meanwhile, the grouping's exports of electrical equipment rose from a total of US$1,000 million in 1996 to US$1,900 million in 1998, after which they shot up to a value of US$10,000 million in 2000 and slipped to US$9,000 million in 2001 (www.aseansec.org). The overall sharp increase in exports of computers, machinery and electrical equipment reflects the new trend in China–ASEAN economic relations. Thus, by no means can it be said that the reallocation of Japanese FDI is a zero-sum game for ASEAN.[12]

Cooperation at the sub-regional level should provide China and Japan with still more areas in which they can cooperate with ASEAN. Currently, the major area for cooperation is the Great Mekong Sub-regional project (GMS). In 1996, ASEAN adopted a basic framework for Mekong basin development cooperation that aims to strengthen the economic linkages between the ASEAN member states and the Mekong-riparian countries (Basic Framework). An important project for ASEAN+3 cooperation, it has drawn on the cooperation of both China and Japan. China is directly linked to the area and thus has a strong interest in participating, while Japan, as the largest donor to less developed countries such as Cambodia and Laos, has played an important role in the area's economic development. It is thus imperative that China and Japan should not be competitors in the project.

Japan currently supports two flagship projects in this area. One is an east-west corridor that will benefit Vietnam, Laos, Thailand, and Myanmar, and the other is a second east-west corridor that will connect Cambodia with its neighbors.[13]

---

[12] www.aseansec.org.

[13] Kawaguchi Yoriko (2003). Building Bridges toward Our Future: Initiating for Reinforcing ASEAN Integration. Policy speech.

Both China and Japan have cooperated in improving infra-structure in the region, such as the Kunming–Bangkok highway, so sub-regional cooperation may well become a platform for China–Japan cooperation, based on goodwill and the coordination of efforts in an integrated regional framework.

As a formal process, cooperation among East Asian countries started in 1997 following the financial crisis. A process that has developed well, it is part of the ASEAN+3 formula and includes informal leaders' and ministers' meetings. Economically, it still follows a multi-layered structure, with efforts made by different parties, including the Japan–Singapore Economic Partnership Agreement (JSEPA), Japan–ASEAN CEP, China–ASEAN CEP, China–ASEAN FTA, and the China–Japan–Korea CEP. It seems that time is still needed before these multi-layered processes can be inte-grated into an East Asian approach that will allow the region to finally move towards attaining an East Asian identity. In fact, this author has proposed the early establishment of the Organization of East Asian cooperation (OEAC), so that the cooperation process in the region might be more speedily coordinated and integrated.[14]

China and Japan are considered the two key players in devel-oping and realizing East Asian cooperation and integration. It seems that while they have some interests in common when it comes to developing East Asian cooperation, there remain differ-ences in their goals and approaches. While China would like to see an East Asian FTA in place as early as possible, and is using the China–ASEAN FTA to forge such a grouping, the move is in no way intended to reduce Japanese interests in ASEAN or exclude Japan from East Asia (Okamoto, 2003).[15] Japan, meanwhile, seems

---

[14] Zhang Yunling (2002). *East Asian Cooperation: Progress and Future*. Beijing: World Affairs Press.

[15] It is said that Tokyo's rapid pursuit of a Japan–ASEAN Comprehensive Economic Partnership (JACEP) was in response to Beijing's proposal for a China–ASEAN FTA, and that Tokyo feared that the tide would shift against it in East Asia. Okamoto (ed.) (2003). *Whither Free Trade Arrangements? Proliferation, Evaluation and Multilateralization*, p. 246. Institute of Developing Economies (IDE) Development Perspective Series.

to have focused its near-term efforts on bilateral rather than regional arrangements. After the conclusion of the JSEPA, Japan concluded a Japan–ASEAN CEP in 2002, but intends to negotiate bilateral FTAs only with the more developed economies of ASEAN, such as Thailand, Malaysia, and the Philippines, rather than with ASEAN en bloc. In Northeast Asia, Japan's priority is to complete a CEP with South Korea, rather than a trilateral one, and its policy regarding an East Asian FTA remains unclear, despite the urging of experts that the government adopt a proactive policy to encourage the establishment of an East Asian economic community by 2007.[16]

Conclusion

A way must now be sought whereby China and Japan can be persuaded to cooperate and move towards East Asian integration. Although their current priorities differ, shared interests can be found since both emphasize the importance of East Asian regional cooperation. In fact, the process of cooperation may well provide the platform necessary for China and Japan to improve their bilateral relations and more readily identify their common interests.

East Asian cooperation and integration is a comprehensive process that would include economic, political, social, and cultural arrangements. China–Japan cooperation in East Asian community-building will certainly require strong political will on both sides. The political foundation for such an endeavor is still very weak and vulnerable because, first, the bilateral relationship is blighted by a historical legacy and security concerns; second, there is a lack of trust regarding the engaging of regional activities because each side considers the other to be a competitor; and third, political barriers make it difficult for the East Asian region to become economically free and a real community. China and Japan must work as partners to forge East Asian cooperation and integration.

---

[16] According to the report, 40 Japanese experts submitted a policy report calling for the establishment of an East Asian economic community.

As regionalism slowly gains strength in East Asia, China is pursuing a policy of promoting regional cooperation and institution building.[17] Starting with economic cooperation, it is hoped that the process will gradually permeate the political, security, social, and cultural mechanisms of the region. It is with this in mind that China's Prime Minister Wen Jiabao called for comprehensive cooperation during the October 2003 ASEAN+3 meeting in Bali.[18] Any process geared to attaining regional cooperation would stand only to benefit from greater Japanese participation and a closer Japan–ASEAN relationship. In fact, since China–ASEAN and Japan–ASEAN relations share a degree of complementarity, China and Japan should work together to provide the leadership so necessary in the region. But if imperatives for cooperation are to prevail and an East Asian community is to be established, both China and Japan need to adopt a new mindset.

---

[17] Chia Siow Yue (2003). "Regional Economic Cooperation in East Asia: Approaches and Process." In *East Asian Cooperation: Progress and Future*. Beijing: World Affairs Press.

[18] *People's Daily* (8 October 2003).

Index